Lighthouses of England
England
The South Coast

The lighthouses of Sussex, Hampshire, the Isle of Wight, Dorset, south Devon and the Channel Islands

Tony Denton and Nicholas Leach

▲ The impressive lighthouse at Portland Bill.

◄ (Front cover) Hurst lighthouse.

◄ (Frontispiece) Point Robert lighthouse on Sark.

Published by
Foxglove Media
Foxglove House
Shute Hill
Lichfield
Staffordshire WS13 8DB
England
Tel (01543) 673594

British Library Cataloguing in Publication Data. A catalogue record for this book is available from the British Library.

ISBN 978-0-95645-6021

Layout and design by Nicholas Leach
Printed by Gomer Press Limited, Llandysul, Ceredigion

Contents

Lighthouse History

This book provides a comprehensive round-the-coast guide to the lighthouses and harbour lights along the south coast of England, covering the counties of Sussex, Hampshire, the Isle of Wight, Dorset and south Devon, as well as Jersey, Guernsey, Alderney and Sark. It starts in East Sussex at Rye Harbour and ends with the numerous lights, large and small, of the Channel Islands. Included are some famous and historically significant lighthouses, with the offshore towers at Eddystone, The Needles and Les Hanois particularly well known.

While the Corporation of Trinity House is responsible for many of these lights, a number of significant harbour lights are in operation in this area, and details of these have been included. This introduction is intended to provide an overview of lighthouse history, development and organisation in England, focusing on the need for lights on the south coast of England, the Channel Islands and the English Channel, as well as explain how Trinity House has developed into the service it is today.

The first lights

Trading by sea has been a principal activity of all civilisations, yet moving goods and cargoes by water involves facing dangers such as storms and bad weather, avoiding reefs, headlands and sandbanks, and making safe passage into ports. The need for aids to navigation is therefore as old as trading

by sea itself and, today, the major offshore lighthouses are supplemented by a plethora of small, locally-operated lights of varying sizes, located around estuaries, piers and ports.

The earliest aids to navigation were beacons or daymarks, sited near harbours rather than on headlands or reefs, to guide ships safely into port. The earliest lighthouses were in the Mediterranean and the oldest such structure of which written records survive was on the island of Pharos, off Alexandra, on the northern coast of Egypt. The Pharos lighthouse, which stood 466ft, was built between 283BC and 247BC and survived to 1326.

The first light on the south coast of England was displayed from the unique medieval lighthouse at St Catherine's Oratory on the Isle of Wight built in 1328 by local squire Walter de Godyton. He was ordered to build the lighthouse and an oratory by the Pope after being threatened with excommunication having been found guilty, together with two associates, of selling wine from a ship which had been wrecked at St Catherine's Point. The wine on the ship was owned by a monastery in Picardy, hence the threat from the Pope.

Ecclesiastical lights such as that at St Catherine's were the first aids to navigation and there are a number of other examples. A light was shown from the chapel or cell of St Petrox at the mouth of the river Dart, and in the fifteenth century a navigation light, which was supposedly maintained by a hermit, was shown from the chapel of St Michael on Rame Head.

As well as the ecclesiastical lights, privately built and funded lighthouses were erected at various locations before the industrial revolution in Britain. The first recorded private proposal for a light was made in 1580 by Gawen Smith, but his intention of placing a beacon on the Goodwin Sands off Kent came to nothing. The earliest privately-funded light on the south coast was that at Eddystone, where the first of five towers to mark the reef was built at the end of the seventeenth century. As the first rock lighthouse, Eddystone is one of the most famous lighthouses.

Another important lighthouse on the south coast that was privately funded was at Portland Bill, marking the western approaches to the English Channel. The Bill extends into the English Channel creating the dangerous currents known as the Portland Race. Sailing ships coming up the Channel could easily be caught out in the Race, particularly if they were unsure of their position. Attempts by Sir John Clayton in 1699 to get a light erected at Portland came to nothing, however, so the

▲ St Catherine's Oratory built in 1328 on one of the highest parts of the Isle of Wight, overlooking the English Channel.

◄ An engraving showing St Catherine's lighthouse on the Isle of Wight as built by Trinity House, before it was reduced in height.

Lighthouse History

HIGHER LIGHTHOUSE, PORTLAN.   W. A. Attwooll's Series.

▲ An old postcard of the high lighthouse at Portland, built in 1869 to replace the original lighthouse, which dated from the early eighteenth century.

merchants of the nearby port of Weymouth petitioned George I in 1716 for a lease from Trinity House to erect a lighthouse. This was granted and two towers were built, being lit for the first time on 29 September 1716. Apart from the Casquets lighthouse of 1724, Portland and Eddystone were the only lights in operation along the south coast during the eighteenth century.

As the south coast was not a particularly busy trade route until the nineteenth century, the aids to navigate along it were relatively few and far between. The development of lighthouses around the British Isles during the last three centuries mirrored the development of trade routes, and the busiest trade routes up to the mid-nineteenth century were elsewhere. The south-east coast was used by vessels trading with Europe, the east coast shipping lanes were frequented by colliers

bringing coal from the industrial north-east to London, and on the west coast Liverpool was the fastest growing port at the time. However, during the second half of the nineteenth century lighthouse provision was greatly expanded and many new stations were built along the south coast as Trinity House gained complete responsibility for lighthouses.

Trinity House

The Corporation of Trinity House is responsible for the operation and maintenance of the major aids to navigation. The exact origins of Trinity House are obscure, but probably date back to the early thirteenth century when groups of tradesmen, such as seamen, masters and pilots, formed guilds to protect their interests. One of the earliest such organisations was the Deptford Trinity House, which was incorporated by Royal

◄ The first high light at Hurst was built in 1786 and was therefore one of the oldest on the south coast. The present tower was built 1867. When the keepers were withdrawn in 1923 the keepers' cottages, pictured in this old photo, were demolished.

Charter after its members had petitioned Henry VIII to prohibit unqualified pilots on the Thames in 1514. Deptford was then a very busy port and the main point of entry for the capital's trade, so pilotage duties were lucrative and Trinity House members wanted to retain their monopoly.

With losses of merchant shipping to London increasing, a series of Orders in Council from the Crown, dating from the early seventeenth century, required Trinity House to build lighthouses on the East Anglian coast to guide vessels through the area's treacherous sandbanks. To maintain the lighthouses, a levy of twelve pence per ton was imposed on ships leaving the ports of Newcastle, Hull, Boston and King's Lynn. However, despite the Crown's Orders, Trinity House was reluctant to build lighthouses and instead encouraged entrepreneurs to consider building them as profit-making undertakings. As a result, private lighthouse ownership

◄ Belle Tout on the cliffs above Beachy Head was operational from 1834 to 1899. Its replacement was part of the improvements to aids to navigation initiated by Trinity House during the nineteenth and twentieth centuries.

Lighthouse History

▶ The lighthouse at Start Point was built in 1836 by Trinity House, at the time the Corporation was becoming fully responsible for the nation's lighthouse management and operation.

▼ Smeaton's Tower from the Eddystone Rock at Plymouth Hoe. After protecting shipping for 120 years, the lighthouse was replaced in 1882 and dismantled stone by stone to be rebuilt on the Hoe.

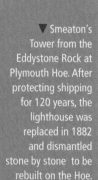

became relatively widespread during the seventeenth century.

Choosing the best position for a light, with sufficiently busy ports nearby from where revenue could be collected, was crucial for the light to yield a good return. Although a proliferation of unnecessary lights was prevented by the involvement of Trinity House, which had to grant permission for a lighthouse to be built, private light owners gained a reputation for greed and lights were built around the coast on a somewhat haphazard basis. As a result, large areas remained unlit, and by the nineteenth century, with the level of trade increasing as industry grew, the situation had become unacceptable to shipowners and mariners.

Trinity House had to react to new demands for better aids to navigation, and with the leases expiring on many private lighthouses the Corporation was forced to take over. In 1807 Trinity House assumed

responsibility for the Eddystone light off Plymouth, and the next three decades saw great changes to lighthouse organisation in England and Wales.

These changes were formalised in an Act of Parliament which was passed in 1836. The Act centralised lighthouse management under the jurisdiction of Trinity House, abolished privately-owned or leased lighthouses, and gave Trinity House complete authority over all aids to navigation. The Corporation became the body to which others had to apply when deciding upon the position and character of lights, as well as when altering or laying down navigation buoys.

The Act gave also Trinity House the power to compulsorily purchase privately-owned lights. Although only a few lighthouses remained in private ownership by the 1830s, the compensation paid to owners by the Corporation was a staggering £1,182,546. The

fourteen towers in private hands in 1832 realised £79,676, almost the same amount as collected from the fifty-five towers then under the control of Trinity House.

During the nineteenth century Trinity House took over more or less all the private lighthouses and assumed control of lighthouse maintenance and construction. The second half of the century witnessed the great period of lighthouse construction and expansion, when Victorian engineers and designers constructed and modernised at least fifty stations, with some new notable rock towers built.

All the major lighthouses along the south coast were modernised and improved, and several new stations were constructed to make up for a lack of lighthouses at some points

▲ An aerial view of Les Hanois lighthouse, built in 1862 off the coast of Guernsey and one of the most spectacular of the rock lighthouses around the coasts of the United Kingdom.

◀ The lighthouse at Alderney, completed in 1913, was one of several built along the south coast in the decade before the First World War.

9

Lighthouse History

on the coast. In 1859 a tower was built to mark The Needles at the western tip of the Isle of Wight, and in 1840 a new tower was built at St Catherine's Point at the southern tip of the island. Further west along the coast, at Anvil Point near Swanage, a new lighthouse was built in 1881 to provide a waypoint for vessels using the English Channel. In

the Channel Islands a new rock tower was built at Les Hanois in 1862, while the small islands of Alderney and Sark gained lighthouses built by Trinity House in 1912 and 1913 respectively.

The first decade of the twentieth century also saw several new and impressive lighthouses built along the south coast. In 1902 the Beachy Head station was completed to replace the light on the cliffs at Belle Tout, while in 1905 a new lighthouse was built at Portland Bill, to replace old high and low lights. Finally, in 1906 a small tower was built at Berry Head, to the south of Brixham, completing a chain of south coast beacons.

Harbour lights

As well as the major lighthouses operated by Trinity House, the south coast has numerous smaller lights, most of which mark the entrances to ports and harbour. Although less well known than the major Trinity House lights such as the Needles,

Eddystone and Beachy Head, they are no less important. These smaller lights have developed in response to specific local circumstances, so their design and purpose differ markedly, and their variety is considerable.

Many harbour authorities are responsible for their own aids to navigation, and a variety of lights and beacons have been erected. Some ports, where vessels need to follow channels, have leading or range lights which mark a safe passage, such as in Plymouth Sound. Others have piers or breakwaters, the limits of which need marking, such as Brixham and St Peter Port, which has a particularly fine tower on the harbour's Castle breakwater.

Automation

The most significant change to lighthouse operation during the twentieth century was the withdrawal of the lightkeeper and the automation of every lighthouse. The lightkeeper once played an essential role in maintaining the light, but during the latter half of the twentieth century the era of manned lighthouses came to an end as automation became the norm.

The idealised view of lighthouse keepers conjures up a romantic image of men living

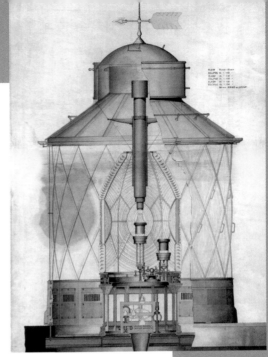

▲ The original Casquets lantern and optic.

▼ The castle at the entrance to Dartmouth harbour from which a light was shown between 1856 and 1864.

▲ The Dogsnest Beacon is situated to the east of St Helier harbour entrance, and is typical of the small aids to navigation which mark the entrance to the area's ports.

▼ St Catherine's lighthouse, which was automated in 1997, is one of several along the south coast where the old keepers' cottages are used as holiday lets.

in a tower with only the sea for company. While this was true for the remote rock stations such as Les Hanois and The Needles, where keepers were confined to fairly cramped quarters for weeks at a time, the reality for most keepers was a little different. Lights on the mainland, such as Portland, had a senior keeper who would be supported by two assistant keepers, usually with families. Under automation, the lights are controlled from a central location and a local attendant looks after the general maintenance during weekly visits.

Aids to navigation continue to improve, and every five years a comprehensive review of navigational requirements around the British Isles is carried out by the General Lighthouse Authorities (GLAs) of the United Kingdom and Ireland, namely Trinity House, the Northern Lighthouse Board and the Commissioners of Irish Lights

Trinity House is constantly reviewing the country's aids to navigation, and, as part of the 2010 review, which included plans to increase the range of a number of lighthouses, the Corporation also proposed to discontinue six others. Those facing closure were Beachy Head, Orfordness, Blacknore Point, Skokholm, Hartland Point and Maryport. With ever more advanced electronic equipment being carried by vessels, even smaller ones, and satellite navigation systems making ships' voyages safer and easier, these lighthouses were deemed to be no longer necessary.

South coast lighthouses

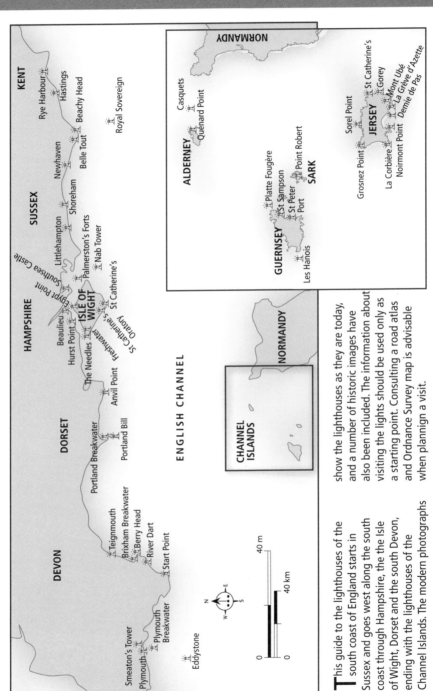

KENT

Rye Harbour
Hastings
Beachy Head
Royal Sovereign

SUSSEX

Newhaven
Belle Tout
Shoreham
Littlehampton
Palmerston's Forts
Nab Tower
St Catherine's

Southsea Castle
Egypt Point
ISLE OF WIGHT

HAMPSHIRE

Beaulieu
Hurst Point
St Catherine's Oratory
Freshwater
The Needles
Anvil Point

DORSET

Portland Breakwater
Portland Bill

DEVON

Teignmouth
Brixham Breakwater
Berry Head
River Dart
Start Point

Smeaton's Tower
Plymouth
Plymouth Breakwater
Eddystone

ENGLISH CHANNEL

CHANNEL ISLANDS

NORMANDY

NORMANDY

ALDERNEY
Casquets
Quénard Point

GUERNSEY
Platte Fougère
St Sampson
St Peter Port
Point Robert
SARK
Les Hanois

Sorel Point
Grosnez Point
JERSEY
St Catherine's
Gorey
Mont Ubé
La Grève d'Azette
La Corbière
Noirmont Point
Demie de Pas

---

40 m

40 km

N
W E
S

0

0

This guide to the lighthouses of the south coast of England starts in Sussex and goes west along the south coast through Hampshire, the the Isle of Wight, Dorset and the south Devon, ending with the lighthouses of the Channel Islands. The modern photographs show the lighthouses as they are today, and a number of historic images have also been included. The information about visiting the lights should be used only as a starting point. Consulting a road atlas and Ordnance Survey map is advisable when plannign a visit.

Rye Harbour

ESTABLISHED
1864

DISCONTINUED
1970

ACCESS
No trace remains of the lighthouse, but leading lights run from the harbour entrance along the channel

Rye became one of the Cinque Ports in the fourteenth century and today its harbour, which is situated halfway between the town and sea three quarters of a mile inland, is tidal. In 1864 the harbour master erected two lights on masts 930 yards apart. These lights were coded to indicate the depth of water in the harbour.

By the nineteenth century, the rear light had been replaced by a 20ft concrete tower, which exhibited lights by night and balls and flags by day. This tower was destroyed in 1918 and was replaced by a hexagonal 40ft concrete tower with the old lights displayed from two windows. The light configuration indicated the depth of water over the bar. This light was demolished in about 1970, and in 1971 was replaced by an occulting white and green light on a tripod.

The front light was replaced by a quick-flashing green light on a square structure on the end of the east pier, which is submerged at spring tides. Today the depth of water over the bar is signalled from the roof of the harbour master's office.

► This lighthouse at Rye Harbour was in use from circa 1918 until 1970. The lights were displayed from the two windows at the top of the concrete tower and were visible for three miles.

Although the town of Hastings has no harbour, a large beach-launched fishing fleet operates from the shingle beach area know as the Stade. As an aid to navigation to guide the vessels back to the beach, the local authority maintains a pair of range lights. The rear range is a white-painted pentagonal close board structure on a concrete base with a sloping roof and pinnacle within West Hill recreational area, off Wellington Road, overlooking the town. Although only 20ft tall, the tower is in an elevated position which gives the light a focal plane of 160ft. Its fixed red light, shown through three elliptical windows, has a range of four miles.

The front range is a simple fixed red light mounted on a 20ft tower structure 1,170 yards away on the seafront, with a range of four miles.

ESTABLISHED
Unknown

OPERATOR
Local council

ACCESS
Both lights can be approached on foot, and the rear range is in a park overlooking the town

◀ The wooden white-painted lighthouse on the west side of Hastings Old Town.

Royal Sovereign

ESTABLISHED
1875

CURRENT TOWER
1971

AUTOMATED
1994

OPERATOR
Trinity House

ACCESS
No public access is allowed onto the platform itself, but trips to the site can be undertaken from Sovereign Harbour at Eastbourne

From as early as the eighteenth century lightvessels have marked the many shoals and sandbanks that stretch as far as twenty miles out to sea off England's south and east coasts. Because of their high maintenance costs, they have been continually reviewed and while some have been retained, others have been replaced by buoys. One, however, Royal Sovereign, situated five and a half miles east of Eastbourne, was replaced by a fixed light.

The first lightvessel to mark the shoal was placed in position in 1875, and in 1966 Trinity House investigated the feasibility of a steel light tower to replace it. The lowest tender was for a concrete structure and so, in 1967, a tender was let to Christiani and Nielson. The concrete base tower was constructed in two sections on the beach near Newhaven, and in 1970 the lower section was sunk onto the bank with a smaller diameter inner section mounted on hydraulic rams inside. The rectangular service and accommodation section was also constructed ashore and, when completed, towed out and positioned on the centre section, which was then jacked up 40ft and locked in position.

The light tower, painted white with a horizontal red band, was constructed of steel and is located on one corner of the roof of the living quarters. The whole structure is 130ft high with the light 92ft above mean high water. The top of the lantern is adorned with aerials, including radar, which are used to monitor shipping. Initially the light was diesel-powered with its rotating flashing white light visible for twenty-eight miles. However, when automated and demanned in 1994, it was converted to solar power with the range reduced to twelve miles.

▶▶ The concrete lighthouse erected in 1971 to mark the Royal Sovereign Shoal replaced a lightvessel which had marked the shoal since 1875.

▶ The cabin and tower after completion being positioned on pontoons ready for installation on site.

Beachy Head

▶▶ Beachy Head
lighthouse seen
from the cliffs.

▼ The lighthouse as
depicted in a hand-
tinted postcard.

The first lighthouse to guide mariners past the dangerous Beachy Head was that at Belle Tout, described below, but when that had to be abandoned at the end of the nineteenth century, Trinity House turned its attention to an alternative site and eventually chose one at the foot of the cliffs at Beachy Head for a lighthouse built to the design of Sir Thomas Matthews. While Belle Tout was inoperable and before the new tower was ready, Trinity House stationed a lightvessel off the Head, complete with its own fog siren apparatus.

Matthews specified the new lighthouse was to be about a mile and a quarter to the east of the Belle Tout tower and approximately 700ft from the base of the chalk cliff. Prior to the construction of the tower, a large coffer dam was erected to enable the removal of the surplus chalk which had fallen from the cliffs, and this was used to create a firm foundation. A steel wire was also erected from a steel platform on the shore to another on the top of the cliff so that the pre-formed granite blocks could be lowered down the cliff on a bogie. They had been shaped in Cornish quarries, brought to Eastbourne by train and driven to the site by traction engines.

The 142ft tapering tower with gallery and lantern was completed in 1902 and was made up of twenty-six courses of interlocking granite masonry infilled with tons of concrete. The masonry courses were built in a stepped formation to a height 45ft above the chalk base rock. The tower, with its seven floors, was painted white with a broad black horizontal band. The large landing stage and base of the tower were left unpainted.

The lantern was supplied and fitted by Chance Brothers of Birmingham. The enormous first order assembly stood 27ft from the galley level to the horizontal centre of the wind vane, and it was more than 15ft in diameter. Chance Brothers also installed first order dioptric apparatus, which consisted of three double panels of optimcal lenses just over four tons in weight floating on a tray of mercury. A clockwork

Beachy Head and Lighthouse 311

Beachy Head

▲ Beachy Head lighthouse with its predecessor, Belle Tout, on the cliffs.

▶▶ Beachy Head lighthouse is one of the most famous along the south coast, but the cliffs behind are constantly being eroded and cliff falls are regular occurrences. The GLA Aids to Navigation Review 2010-15 recommended that six lighthouses should be discontinued, of which Beachy Head was one.

mechanism was used to turn the lens. Beachy Head was the first English lighthouse to be fitted with a Matthews-designed incandescent oil burner which gave a light of 1,200 candle power that was magnified to 23,000 candle power by the optical apparatus. The last gallery stone was set into position on 25 February 1902 and light was first displayed on 2 October 1902 witha characteristic of two flashes every twenty seconds.

During the Second World War, the light was extinguished unless a request came from the Naval Authorities for it to be shown to guide aircraft home. This caused a problem as it took almost fifteen minutes to light the paraffin vapour burner. To overcome this, a keeper had the idea of removing the burner and illuminating the light by placing the kitchen light on a temporary wooden platform. It did not give a full light but was sufficient to be seen from an aircraft. As the light was probably only required for at most five minutes, it was easy to extinguish it quickly.

In 1975 an electricity cable was erected from the cliff top and the tower provided with electrical power. The paraffin burner and explosive fog gun were replaced with electrical units and now the light, which gives a flash every twenty seconds, is visible for twenty miles and the foghorn sounds every thirty seconds.

The only drama to occur since then was in 1999, when a cliff fall severed the electricity supply to the tower. A temporary generator was installed on a platform until new cables could be supplied and fitted. The system was modernised at the same time, with new lamps, fog signals and emergency lights.

Belle Tout

ESTABLISHED
1828

CURRENT TOWER
1834

DISCONTINUED
1899

OPERATOR
Private residence

ACCESS
The lighthouse is on the downs and is easily approached via the coast road

▲ Belle Tout lighthouse seen when in operation.

▶▶ The famous Belle Tout lighthouse has had a chequered history, including being used in 1986 by the BBC for the making of Fay Weldon's drama, Life and Loves of a She-Devil.

The cliffs of Beachy Head stand as one of the main dangers to shipping using the Channel. The first attempts to mark them as such may have been a beacon on the cliffs near Eastbourne used around 1670, but documentary evidence of this is scant and further aids to navigation in the area were few and far between with the Owers lightvessel, stationed off Selsey in 1788, the only help for mariners on the East Sussex coast until the 1800s.

In 1828 a local man, known as 'Mad Jack' Fuller, built a temporary wooden lighthouse on the cliffs three miles west of Eastbourne at Belle Tout under the auspices of Trinity Corporation. It came into operation on 1 October 1828, and proved so successful that an agreement was granted to build a permanent lighthouse.

W. Hallett and James Walker began designing a new lighthouse in 1831 to replace the original temporary structure. Construction work started in 1832 using Aberdeen granite and local limestone, and the Belle Tout lighthouse came into operation on 11 October 1834. The original tower was a 47ft circular granite structure situated 100ft from the cliff edge. The flashing white light, housed in a lantern complete with gallery, was powered by thirty oil lamps and, in clear weather, could be seen for twenty-three miles.

Although the location of the lighthouse was carefully planned so that the light would be obscured by the edge of the cliff, this arrangement was subsequently affected by erosion of the cliffs, which meant that vessels could be on the rocks yet still see the light.

The light itself was far from perfect, and its height above sea level – 250ft – meant it was often obscured by fog and sea mists. In 1899 the Belle Tout light was discontinued and replaced three years later by the current Beachy Head lighthouse at the foot of the cliffs. The Belle Tout light was then sold into private ownership, and during the Second World War, with its owners evacuated, it was damaged by shells fired by Canadian Troops using it as target practice. After the war it was given to Eastbourne Corporation but by the 1960s was once again in private hands.

In 1999, following further erosion, it was only 9ft from the cliff edge. So, in a well-documented move, a new ground floor base was constructed 56ft inland and the tower with its modern two-storey residence was moved onto the new base.

In 2007 Mark and Louise Roberts, who had overseen the moving of the tower, put Belle Tout up for sale for £850,000. The lighthouse was purchased in 2008 by the Belle Tout Lighthouse Co Ltd with the intention of opening it as a bed and breakfast and tourist centre, and during 2009 the building was extensively restored and renovated. In March 2010 the lighthouse was opened for paying guests with themed rooms.

Newhaven

ESTABLISHED
1883

CURRENT TOWER
1891 (west), 2006
(east)

OPERATOR
Newhaven Harbour
Authority

ACCESS
Both the East Pier and
the West Breakwater
are open to the public

►► The lighthouse
at the end of the
west pier dates
from 1883.

▼ The entrance to
Newhaven harbour
looking east towards
the west pier, with
a cross-Channel
steamer departing.

In the 1880s the harbour at Newhaven was substantially improved by the erection of two piers. To aid shipping, lights were erected on each terminus. The lighthouse built in 1883, on the end of the west pier, was a circular stone-built tower, three storeys high, with a lantern and gallery. In 1976 the west pier almost collapsed and the lighthouse suffered damage, so it was demolished shortly afterwards. However, the lantern was saved and is now on display in nearby Paradise Park.

Alongside the lighthouse was a signal tower from which a storm warning cone was hoisted, pointed upwards for a northern wind and downwards for a southern wind. The cone and weather vane from the lighthouse are now in the Newhaven Maritime Museum.

With the completion of the east pier in 1883, an open 40ft wooden lattice tower with a wooden lantern room was erected on its terminus. In 1928 this tower was replaced by a 41ft square steel lattice tower supporting a circular gallery and a hexagonal black lantern with a coned top, which displayed a flashing green light visible for six miles. In the upper section of the lattice tower, a white-painted wooden lookout was constructed.

In 2002 the harbour authority wanted to close the east pier and demolish the light because of vandalism, but this was deferred. By 2005, however, the situation had worsened, and in 2006 the light was demolished. In its place a 41ft circular steel pole was erected, painted white with three horizontal green bands near the top. A round steel plate on top supports a light displaying an isophase green light showing every ten seconds visible for four and half miles.

SIGNAL STATION, NEWHAVEN

Newhaven

▶ The channel marker is housed in this small wooden hut on the west bank of the river.

▶▶ The old East Pier light, built in 1928, was demolished in 2006.

The entry into the harbour was substantially improved in 1891 when the long breakwater was completed, and a 45ft circular cast-iron lighthouse was erected on its terminus. It was painted white with two red horizontal stripes and red railings round its gallery, and displays a white isophase light every ten seconds visible for twelve miles from a white circular lantern with an ornate domed top.

Entry into the inner harbours is marked by two sets of navigation lights on simple poles. The two east ones each show two vertical fixed green lights, and the two west ones two vertical fixed red ones. The channel to the inner berths is marked by a channel marker mounted in a wooden shed situated between the Hope Inn and the yacht club.

In September 2009 the future of Newhaven Port was discussed but proposals, which included the possibility of berthing arrangements for larger ferries, will not have any effect on the navigational light arrangements.

▶ The light at the end of the east pier erected in 2006 with a steel plate on top supporting a simple polycarbonate light displaying an isophase green light.

Shoreham

Although Shoreham was a port in Roman times, it was not until 1816 that the cut which now forms the entrance to the harbour was excavated, and not until 1957 were the two breakwaters constructed to protect the entrance from the build-up of shingle. Although eleven aids to navigation are operational in the port, only one can be described as a lighthouse, and that is situated at the side of the main road near the lifeboat house and middle pier.

Built in 1846, the unpainted 42ft circular limestone tower has an ornate black lantern and balcony. In 1985 the lantern was completely refurbished. Its flashing white light is visible for ten miles and operates in conjunction with a front light located on the end of the middle pier 200 yards away. This light, housed in a square black box, is on a white 6ft lattice tower on the roof of Shoreham Port Authority watchtower. This two-storey white building also supports the harbour foghorn and traffic control lights. The white flashing light, visible for nine miles, is supplemented by red and green navigation lights.

When, in 1957, the two breakwaters were built out from the harbour entrance, a 10ft-high concrete column with a simple light was erected on each outer end. On the east breakwater its green column shows a green flashing light visible for eight miles and on the west its red column shows a red flashing light visible for four miles.

ESTABLISHED
1846

CURRENT TOWER
1846

OPERATOR
Shoreham Port Authority

ACCESS
The lighthouse is on the seafront on open land, but the other lights are visible only from a distance as access around the port is restricted

▲ The nineteenth century lighthouse at Shoreham.

◄ The lighthouse stands on open ground close to the lifeboat station.

Littlehampton

Although there has been an anchorage in the river Arun at Littlehampton since Roman times, it was not until the seventeenth century that the first wharf, Old Quay Wharf, was erected and the development of the port began. Further wooden wharfs were constructed with the first of the piers, the east pier, erected in 1860s.

In 1848 a light, supported by a 40ft high white square pyramidal wooden tower with a green cupola roof, was erected at a point which, at a later date, was to be the start of the east pier. Visible for ten miles, this light, which looked like a pepper pot, became the rear range for a new front range, which was erected in 1868 on the end of the east pier. At 26ft high, this light was mounted on a similar structure to the rear light and as a result the two lights came to be known as 'salt and pepper'.

In 1940 they were demolished to avoid the enemy using them as navigational aids. But at the end of the war it was decided to resurect them, so in 1948 a pair of lights was built in the same location. The rear range is a 23ft unpainted circular concrete column with four tapered buttresses complete with a circular concrete lantern. The light is displayed through an envelope opening near the top. It has a white sector over the channel with an occulting character, six seconds on, and one and a half seconds eclipse, with a range of nine miles. There is a yellow sector, which shines to the south south west over the training wall.

The front range, on the end of the east pier, was replaced by a simple fixed green light visible for seven miles on a 10ft high black column. In 1848 a simple flashing red light, visible for six miles, mounted on a black metal pole was erected on the end of the west pier. Operated by the Littlehampton Harbour Board, the rear light is on the waterfront, but the two pier lights are not accessible. Recently, considerable improvements have taken place in the harbour with the old wooden wharfs being replaced by concrete and steel structures.

▲ The wooden tower of 1848 at the east side of the harbour entrance.

▶▶ The modern lighthouse at Littlehampton dates from 1948.

▶ The original lights marking the entrance to the harbour were demolished during the Second World War.

PIER AND HARBOUR MOUTH, LITTLEHAMPTON.

Southsea Castle

ESTABLISHED
1822

CURRENT TOWER
1822

OPERATOR
Portsmouth Harbour
Authority

ACCESS
The lighthouse is in
the castle, which is
open daily from April
to September, with an
entrance fee payable

Southsea Castle was the last of Henry VIII's coastal defences to be constructed. Built in 1544, it had various periods of decay and restoration until the 1820s, when it was substantially rebuilt. As part of the work, at the request of the Admiralty, a lighthouse was erected on the north side of the western gun platform on the Western Ramparts, built into one of the outer walls.

The 30ft cylindrical stone tower, which was commissioned in 1822, has a gallery and lantern room with a pagoda roof and is white with black bands. Situated between Clarence and South Parade piers, it guides ships through the deep water approaches to the busy harbour.

The tower displays a flashing white light, which is visible for eleven miles, with three fixed lights, white, red and green, to mark different channels. The lighthouse can be seen from outside the castle, but a view of the base can only be seen by entry to the site. Although an active light, it is a listed building and part of the castle site.

▶ The Southsea
lighthouse is built
into one of the walls
of the castle.

Palmerston's Forts

In the nineteenth century Lord Palmerston sanctioned the building of a series of forts in the channel between Portsmouth and the Isle of Wight to protect the naval dockyard from attack. Of five proposed forts, only four were completed. Spitbank Fort, which guarded Spithead, was the nearest to Portsmouth with Horse Sand Fort to the south-east. The other forts, No Man's Land and St Helens, were built to the north east and east of the Isle of White.

The forts were designed by Captain E. H. Stewart with the metalwork designed separately by Captain Inglis and Lieut English. Under the supervision of Sir John Hawkshaw, work began in 1861 but was suspended in April 1862. It recommenced in March 1864 and by March 1880 they were all completed. During the early 1900s submarine defences were built from Horse Sand Fort to Southsea and from No Man's Land Fort to Ryde Sands forcing all large shipping to travel between the two forts.

The forts were built to repel a French invasion, but as this never happened they were subsequently referred to as 'Palmerston's Follies'. However, they were later used during the Second World War and today carry aids to navigation to assist vessels entering Portsmouth.

SPITBANK FORT • Spitbank was commenced in March 1861 but it was not completed until June 1878, although the lighthouse on the fort was built in 1866. The fort is circular in plan, 165ft in diameter with walls 48ft thick, and stands on sea-bed foundation walls of eight-ton concrete blocks. Below basement level is filled with shingle topped by a 10ft thick concrete slab. Above the basement is a main floor which supported the guns with the lighthouse and observation post on the roof.

The 24ft red circular tower with a red lantern shows a flashing red light every five seconds visible for seven miles.

SPITBANK FORT

ESTABLISHED
1866

CURRENT TOWER
1866

OPERATOR
Spitbank Fort Ltd

ACCESS
The fort can be visited by boat for; boats leave Gosport, The Historic Dockyard and The Hard at Portsmouth

HORSE SAND FORT

ESTABLISHED
1865

CURRENT TOWER
1865

ACCESS
Only by boat

▼ An old photo of Spitbank Fort, which is situated near the entrance to Portsmouth harbour about half a mile south of Southsea.

Palmerston's Forts

▶ Spitbank Fort with Horse Sand Fort in the background.

▼ No Man's Land Fort lies between Horse Sand Fort and the Isle of Wight.

It is perched on top of a white service building on the southern aspect of the fort.

The ownership of the fort has changed several times after it was declared surplus to requirements in 1962 by the Admiralty and sold to a private buyer in 1982. It was sold again in 2009 and during 2010 was under renovation with a planned reopening by 2011.

HORSE SAND FORT • Built at a cost of £424,694 and situated about two miles south-east of Spitbank Fort, Horse Sand Fort was built between 1865, when foundations of large concrete blocks with an outer skin of granite blocks were laid, and 1880. The interior was filled with clay and shingle, and covered with a thick layer of concrete. This and No Man's Land fort are the two largest forts, measuring 240ft in diameter with foundation walls 59ft thick. Horse Sand is slit into three levels with the top section supporting a lighthouse as well as chimneys and ventilators.

The Fort's aid to navigation is now a light with an elevation of 69ft showing a green light, one second on, one second eclipse, mounted on a short mast. Unlike the other forts, which were sold in the 1980s, Horse Sand Fort was retained by the Admiralty but has lain derelict ever since.

NO MAN'S LAND FORT • Built at a cost of £462,500, No Man's Land Fort is situated about a mile north-east of Ryde. It was started in 1867 and completed in 1880, and is identical in basic construction to Horse Sand Fort at 240ft diameter with three floors. The lighthouse on top, commissioned in 1880, was a 33ft white octagonal tower with a gallery and lantern, with a pitched roof dwelling for the keepers attached. The lantern was subsequently removed, and the isophase red light showing every three seconds was shown from a pole atop the tower. In 2010 this light was deactivated.

The fort was sold to a private owner in 1982 and converted into a top-class hotel with luxuries including an indoor swimming pool and two helipads. In 2004 an outbreak of legionella caused it to close and the fort

was put up for sale. In March 2009 it was sold again, this time fetching £910,000.

ST HELENS FORT • Situated about a mile off the coast, opposite Bembridge harbour on the Isle of Wight, to protect St Helens Road anchorage, St Helens Fort is the most southerly of the Palmerston Forts. Work began on the Fort in 1867, and the structure was smaller than the other Solent forts. Costing £123,110, it was built using a variety of local stones, and was concrete-faced with granite blocks and stonework.

Oval in shape, it is 135ft at its broadest point and 40ft above the sea bed. Because of the soft ground on which it was built, a ring of iron caissons was sunk into the sea bed to form a firm foundation. However, despite this, the fort took on a lean, so the plans were altered to ensure the load was centred on the foundation. This meant it was 1880 before it was completed.

Although the Fort was built as a defensive structure, a white

23ft square pyramidal tower was erected on the top to support a white square box which housed a white navigation light. Operated privately, the light displays three white flashes every ten seconds and is visible for eight miles.

The fort was sold into private hands in the 1980s and was again on the market in 2003 including planning permission for a private dwelling, with offers over £200,000 sought. Although the fort is normally inaccessible on foot, an annual trek at low spring tides is undertaken on an ad hock basis using the shingle causeway running from St Helens or Bembridge harbour.

▲ St Helen's Fort, situated opposite Bembridge harbour, displays a small navigation light.

◄ The remains of a twelfth century church tower on the foreshore at St Helens are painted for use as a seamark. When the church ceased to be used in 1703, the tower was bricked up and the seaward wall painted white.

Beaulieu

ESTABLISHED
2000

CURRENT TOWER
2000

OPERATOR
Royal Cruising Club
Pilotage Foundation

ACCESS
From Lepe Country
Park, on the corner by
the entrance to the
Cruising Club

▶▶ The Beaulieu
River Millennium
Beacon marks the
entrance to the river.

▼ The modern
Beaulieu
lighthouse stands
in the grounds of
Lepe House.

The lighthouse at Beaulieu, the newest in Britain, is called Beaulieu River Millennium Beacon. Its construction came about following concerns expressed by a local committee working in association with Trinity House, which looked at ways to improve the aids to navigation in the river where the Lepe joined the Solent. The committee, made up of Harbour Master John Edward and experienced local sailors, wanted to not only improve navigation into the river, but also to celebrate the millennium with a permanent structure.

After much debate, they decided to provide a traditional lighthouse. A suitable location was found opposite the river entrance in the grounds of Lepe House, whose owner, Mr Pease, donated a plot of land in his garden. The lighthouse, designed by local architect Brian Turner and built by local contractor Mark Keeping, was commissioned on 8 July 2000 by Lord Lieutenant of Hampshire, Mrs Mary Fagan, in the presence of Lord Montagu and other dignitaries.

The 25ft white tower is made from cement rendered brick, with a concrete gallery. The octagonal lamp room consists of glass panels with a fibre-reinforced composite roof topped by a weather vane. The Tideman ML300 lantern supplied by FPM Henderson Ltd of Glasgow has a directional sector beam showing a white occulting light over a safe channel with red and green sectors on each side. The light, which also acts as a day mark, was financed by local boat owners and the Royal Cruising Club Pilotage Foundation.

Hurst Point

▶▶ The two low lights standing within the walls of Hurst Castle date from 1866 (on right) and 1911.

▼ An old postcard of the high light and acetylene house (to right of tower), near the castle.

Hurst Point lighthouse, situated on the spit of land at Hurst Point, guides vessels through the western approaches to the Solent, indicating the line of approach through the Needles Channel. Although a light was shown on Hurst Point as early as 1733, not until 1781 was a meeting of shipmasters and merchants organised to submit a formal petition to Trinity House for lights in the neighbourhood of the Isle of Wight.

Before they received the patent, Trinity House discussed several draft agreements with William Tatnell, a merchant in London, who projected the lights. In 1785 negotiations with Tatnell fell through and Trinity House erected a lighthouse at Hurst, to the south-west of Hurst Castle, which was lit for the first time on 29 September 1786. However, as this light was obscured to shipping from certain directions, an additional light was constructed, which also served as a guiding line

to vessels. Designed by Daniel Alexander, the high light, as it became known, was first shown on 27 August 1812.

Extensive additions were made to the castle between 1865 and 1873 necessitating the repositioning of the lights. A new low light was erected on the castle's defence wall, reached by a staircase built outside the fort. The 1812 high lighthouse was moved 50ft east and, with new cottages, relit in September 1867. This 85ft tower is still operational today, with its light visible for fourteen nautical miles.

The shifting sands of Shingles Bank forced the 1865-built low light to be abandoned and it was discontinued on 30 November 1911. In its place a new low lighthouse was built, in the form of a square metal structure standing on a framework of steel joists attached to the wall of the castle and showing a light visible for twelve miles. The 52ft metal tower was originally painted red but, in 1977, when

Hurst Point

▶ The two low lights at Hurst, with the high light in the background. The 1911 structure (on left) was unusual because it could be moved along the castle walls to mark the ever-shifting Shingles Bank. The keys to the structure were handed over to English Heritage in June 2010 at an event attended by Friends of Hurst Castle and members of the Association of Lighthouse Keepers.

▶▶ The impressive high light at Hurst is a major landmark at the end of the spit.

▼ Hurst lighthouse and the old keepers' cottages are close to Hurst Castle, which dates from the sixteenth century.

it too was decommissioned, it was repainted grey to match the surrounding background and eliminate navigational confusion.

In 1923 the keepers were withdrawn and both operational lights were automated. A major modernisation of the station, prompted by a growth in traffic using the Needles Channel, was completed in July 1997, and following consultation, high intensity projectors were installed. These are exhibited day and night to mark the channel between The Needles and the treacherous Shingles Bank.

Until 2010 the low light was owned by Trinity House, but on 10 June that year its keys were ceremoniously handed over to English Heritage by the Corporation. Deputy Master Rear Admiral Sir Jeremy De Halpert presented the antique keys to Dawn Postlethwaite, Head of Visitor Operations for English Heritage, and the structure was placed under the auspices of the Hurst Castle management.

Nab Tower

ESTABLISHED
1920

CURRENT TOWER
1920

AUTOMATED
1983

OPERATOR
Trinity House

ACCESS
Can only be viewed
by boat

▶▶ Nab Tower
marks the Nab rock
in the deepwater
approach to the
eastern Solent.

▶ The Nab Tower
being towed out
from Shoreham
Harbour shortly
after completion.
The structure was
sunk in position on
13 September 1920
and replaced the
Nab lightvessel.

During the First World War, the Admiralty, concerned about enemy submarines attacking Britain's merchant fleet, planned to build eight fortified steel towers so that a barrier could be formed by stringing nets between them. Although as many as 3,000 men were employed on the project, only one was completed, the Nab Tower, although another was partially finished when the war ended. Of little use as a defence measure, the tower proved an ideal replacement for the Nab Lightship, which was based at the eastern edges of the Spithead approaches. The new light would guide vessels into Portsmouth and Southampton, while the tower would be available as a fortified defence post if necessary.

The structure, designed by G. Menzies, was 40ft in diameter with latticed steel work surrounding a 90ft cylindrical steel tower and was built on a hollow 80ft thick concrete base designed to be flooded and sunk in about twenty fathoms. Shaped with pointed bows and stern for easy towing, it was positioned near the light float in 1920. The sea was let into the base, which caused the tower to sink into position as planned but with a three degree list.

Alteration for use as a lighthouse included the erection of a clockwork-driven red rotating light and a similar white rotating light on round turrets on either side. It was staffed as a rock station until 1983 when an automated acetylene light was erected on a short red octagonal tower with a gallery and lantern near the perimeter and the keepers withdrawn.

Today a helipad and a bank of solar panels occupy the top. In 1995 the station was converted to solar power and the optic was changed to a new propriety lantern by Orga, which shows a flashing white light visible for sixteen miles. The fog signal gives two blasts every thirty seconds audible for two miles. This rather ugly structure, reached by sea, was never given the distinction of being called a lighthouse, and is still referred to as Nab Tower.

Nab Light Tower BEING TOWED FROM SHOREHAM.

St Catherine's Oratory

The history of the lighthouses as St Catherine's Point starts as early as the fourteenth century in peculiar circumstances. Lord of Chale, Walter de Godyton, was caught plundering wine from the wreck of St Marie of Bayonne in Chale Bay off Atherfield on 20 April 1313. As a punishment, he was instructed to build a lighthouse and an oratory, where priests could pray for the souls of the lost sailors.

Situated on a hilltop at Chale three miles north-west of the current tower, the lighthouse he had built was completed in 1328, a year after Godyton's death. It consisted of a 35ft four-storey stone building, octagonal externally but square internally, with a pyramid top, and is today referred to as the 'Pepper Pot'.

There was already an oratory on the hilltop, dedicated to St Catherine of Alexandria, and the lighthouse was erected to the west of the existing building. However, all that remains of that structure are imprints of the four walls. At the top were eight openings through which a coal-fired light was displayed. It lasted until 1547, when Henry VIII ordered the closure of all Catholic religious institutions.

In the 1700s Sir Richard Worsley, of Appuldurcombe House, bolstered the structure by adding four large buttresses to stop it collapsing, giving it the appearance of a stone space rocket. It is the second oldest lighthouse in the British Isles, after the Pharos at Dover.

With no light to guide vessels, wrecks continued to occur in the seas to the south of the Isle of Wight, and so in 1785 Trinity House decided to resurrect the old light. They began the erection of a new lighthouse, sited close to the earlier one, but a little closer to the sea. Known as the 'salt cellar', the building was never completed, as experience soon showed that the fogs and mists, common throughout the year, rendered the site almost useless as one from which to display an aid to navigation. Even on a fine day with clear skies elsewhere, fog can reduce visibility at the summit to fifty yards. The circular stone base of the planned tower remains.

▶ The incomplete base of the proposed 1785 lighthouse is about seventy yards from the original lighthouse as depicted in this historic postcard of the area.

▲ This foggy scene, taken on a fine summer day, illustrates the reason why the light was never completed. The hilltop is so enshrouded in mist that the original lighthouse, only seventy yards away, is not visible.

◄ This photo of the 1328 lighthouse, taken on a sunny day, shows how the mist made the lighthouse of questionable use.

St Catherine's

ESTABLISHED
1838

CURRENT TOWER
1875

AUTOMATED
1997

OPERATOR
Trinity House

ACCESS
Walk the coast path
from Niton Undercliffe

St Catherine's lighthouse is situated at Niton Undercliffe. This impressive lighthouse was built after the building of lights on the hilltop at Chale, three miles away, had proved unworkable, as described above. Two factors combined to see the building of a new lighthouse on a new site. Firstly, the sailing ship Clarendon was wrecked on rocks nearby on 11 October 1836, with the loss of almost all her passengers and crew. As she was just the latest of many wrecks in the area, with more than sixty ships lost in Chale Bay between 1746 and 1808, improvements in naviagtion were clearly needed.

Secondly, following the Act of 1836, Trinity House was in a position to address the problem of a lighthouse at St Catherine's Point, which remained a danger to shipping, and chose a natural terrace on the Down on which to construct a tower. No doubt the loss of Clarendon also persuaded the Brethren to act with haste. With a suitable location for the lighthouse chosen, construction work began and an elegant crenellated octagonal tower, 84ft in height, with ninety-four steps up to the lantern, was built to the design of James Walker. It was built up from a base plinth as a three-tier octagon, diminishing by stages, and was completed in ashlar stone rising in a series of tiers. A light was first displayed in March 1840.

However, the elevation of the light proved to be too high as the lantern frequently became enveloped in mist, and so in 1875 it was decided to lower the light 43ft by taking about 19ft out of the uppermost section of the tower and about 24ft out of the middle tier. This made the lighthouse more effective and forms the structure in use today.

The smaller tower, which can be seen in front of the original one, was built in 1932 to accommodate a new fog signal apparatus. The original fog signal had been installed in 1868 in a purpose-built house on the cliff edge, with an additional keeper to maintain it. However, when the

▶▶ The two towers that make up St Catherine's lighthouse are known locally as the 'cow and calf'.

▶ The tower in the early twentieth century, before the smaller fog signal tower was added.

ST. CATHERINE'S LIGHTHOUSE - ISLE of WIGHT. 286.

St Catherine's

▶ St Catherine's lighthouse when it was manned, with the keepers' dwellings in natural stone. The bird perches, visible just beneath the lantern, were installed in 1913 and the fog horn was built in 1932, so the perches were there for at least twenty years.

▼ St Catherine's lighthouse is situated at the southernmost tip of the Isle of Wight, off the A3055, five miles west of Ventnor, and has a commanding view over the English Channel.

building was undermined by cliff erosion it had to be replaced, and so a secondary tower was built. The fog signal was discontinued in 1987 and replaced by a radio beacon transmitter.

St Catherine's was automated in 1997, with the keepers leaving the lighthouse on 30 July that year. Today, the main light, of 5.25 million candela and visible for up to thirty nautical miles in clear weather, is the third most powerful in Trinity House

service and guides shipping in the Channel as well as vessels approaching the Solent. A fixed red subsidiary light, displayed from a window 23ft below the main light, faces westward over Atherfield Ledge. This was first shown in 1904 and has a range of seventeen miles.

The lighthouse complex is one of Trinity House's Visitor Centres, and it is open to the public for guided tours at various times between February and October.

Freshwater

ESTABLISHED
1785

DISCONTINUED
1859

DEMOLISHED
circa 1913

To the west of the Isle of Wight, The Needles form a narrow chalky peninsula extending out from Freshwater Gate, which rises from jagged rocks to over 400ft. These rocks have always been a hazard to ships passing up the Solent to Portsmouth and Southampton. Because of the dangers of the channel into the Solent, shipping often avoided the western approaches and rounded the Isle of Wight from the east. To improve the situation, in 1781 shipowners petitioned Trinity House to build a lighthouse.

Although approval was given in 1782, Trinity House did not begin work on a lighthouse until 1785. Consultant engineer at the time, Samuel Wyatt, recommended Richard Japp be commissioned to carry out the work on the cliffs overlooking The Needles. The resulting structure was of a similar design to Hurst Castle and St Catherine's Point. The small 22ft circular brick tower with a lantern on top and an attached keepers' dwelling was situated on top of a cliff overhanging Scratchell's Bay.

Called Freshwater lighthouse, although often referred to as Needles Tower, it was first lit on 29 September 1786 but the light, which was 475ft above sea level, was often obscured by mist and fog and thus proved to be of somewhat limited use. The experiment of using ten Argand lamps and eighteen-inch parabolic reflectors, designed to give improved light with an alleged visibility of eleven miles, did not solve the problem so Trinity House decided a new light had to be built at sea level, on the outer extremity of The Needles range of rocks.

As a result the Freshwater lighthouse was extinguished on 1 January 1859. It was initially planned that it would be demolished as soon as the new light was exhibited, but it was reported as being in existence as a landmark as late at 1913. There is, however, no trace of it today.

◀ The original lighthouse to mark The Needles and the western extremity of the Isle of Wight was at Freshwater, but it was demolished a century ago.

The Needles

ESTABLISHED
1859

CURRENT TOWER
1859

AUTOMATED
1994

OPERATOR
Trinity House

ACCESS
By boat, and can be
viewed from cliffs

The lighthouse at The Needles dates from the middle of the nineteenth century, a time when lighthouse building by Trinity House was at its height. The Needles, a line of chalk rocks, is situated at the western extremity of the Isle of Wight. In order to effectively mark the area, close to which lies the treacherous submerged Goose Rock that is liable to catch out the unwary mariner, plans were drawn up during the 1850s for a light nearer to sea level than the existing Freshwater light situated on the cliff top.

In 1853 Trinity House instructed its consultant engineer, James Walker, to prepare the plans, specifications and estimates for erecting a new tower, which was to be positioned near to sea level on the outermost rock, or 'Needle'. Work began on 26 July 1857 when local stonemasons and quarrymen began the construction of the tower. The chalk of the Needles Point rock was excavated by the workforce of Thomas Ormiston with the men standing for almost the whole time in sea water.

After eight weeks of hard labour, the 3ft thick granite foundation, measuring 38ft in diameter, had been set in place to form the base of the tower. Much of the base rock was cut away to form the foundation, and cellars and storehouses were excavated in the chalk.

The tower, 102ft tall, was constructed during 1858 of granite blocks, most of which were dovetailed together. The tower had perpendicular sides and was of uniform diameter, with an unevenly stepped base designed to prevent the seas from sweeping up the tower. For almost a century it had a black band, gallery and lantern to give it added visibility against the . white rock face. The interior was divided into five apartments: the ground floor was used as the oil room; the next floor was for the provisions; the next

▶▶ The Needles lighthouse has, since 1987, supported a helipad. Walker's lanterns have trapezoid glazing while the helideck had square or diamond-shaped girders.

▶ The lighthouse before the helicopter platform had been added. The wall of the tower varies from 3ft 6in in thickness at the entrance to 2ft at the top.

The Needles

▲ The lighthouse and its surroundings seen from the air, before the helicopter platform had been added to the tower.

▶▶ The Needles tower, dating from 1859, had the helipad built above the lantern in the 1980s. During the Second World War, the lighthouse was used for target practise by the gunners of German aircraft, and the tower was hit on several occasions by machine gun fire.

▶ The Needles is a well-known landmark at the western tip of the Isle of Wight, west of Alum Bay.

level contained the kitchen, above which was a purpose-built bedroom with bunks and wardrobes, and the floor above was the service room, which gave access to the lantern. When on duty the keepers spent the majority of their time here.

The whole undertaking had cost almost £20,000 and the light was first displayed on 22 May 1859. The original lantern was fitted by H. Wilkins & Son, of London, and it contained a first order dioptric lens apparatus by Chance Brothers, of Smethwick, and multi-wicked oil burner. Complaints were made soon after the light was first shown that it was not bright enough, so the situation was quickly remedied with the fitting of various coloured panels of glass to the lantern in place of a shade.

The second order Fresnel lens currently displays an occulting white light with red and green sectors to mark the safe channel. The light has two white sectors, two red and one green, with one of the red sectors intensified.

The red intensified sector marks the St Anthony Rocks; the white sector marks the approach to the Needles Channel from the west; another red sector marks the Shingles Bank; another white sector marks the course through the Needles Channel; and the green sector marks a safe channel past the Hatherwood Rocks and the Warden Ledge. A foghorn gives two sounds every thirty seconds.

Since its construction, various alterations to the lighthouse have been made. The most recent was the addition of a helipad, built on top of the lighthouse in 1987. The station was automated in 1994 and the keepers left for the last time on 8 December that year.

In 2010 work was undertaken to reinforce the base of the tower. Storm and wave action had damaged the protective capping at the base of the tower, exposing the foundations. The remedial works involved replacing the protective capping with a steel-reinforced concrete covering, toed into the rock.

Egypt Point

Situated on the most northerly point of the Isle of Wight, at Egypt Point on the promenade at West Cowes, is an aid to navigation of unique design. Erected in 1897, the tower houses an electrically-powered white light which is visible for ten miles and consists of a rotating optic in a white circular lantern. It is mounted on a red pedestal on a white eighteen-inch round box on a red post. At its base is a white square plinth from which guy rods steady the lantern box. The lower section is surrounded by white railings and there is an external ladder up to the lantern.

The whole 25ft structure is mounted on a concrete plinth built out from the promenade retaining wall. To avoid dazzling the traffic on the roadway, two metal flaps were welded onto the top of the upper housing. The light was managed by Trinity House, but was deactivated in 1989 and in 1997 handed over to the local council. The light can be easily visited either on foot or by car by travelling along the promenade from West Cowes.

After the original lantern was removed from the tower, it was displayed at the Trinity House Lighthouse Museum in Penzance. When that closed the lantern was removed and renovated and now stands outside the Trinity House display at Hurst Castle.

ESTABLISHED	1897
CURRENT TOWER	1897
DISCONTINUED	1989
OPERATOR	Trinity House
ACCESS	Via the promenade from West Cowes

◀ The original lantern from Egypt Point on display at Hurst Castle. The light was improved in 1925 when it was converted to acetylene operation.

▼ The unusual light at Egypt Point faces the Solent at the most northerly point of the Isle of Wight.

Anvil Point

▶▶ The squat
lighthouse at Anvil
Point marking a
passage along the
English Channel.

▼ Anvil Point
lighthouse is sited
on the cliffs to the
west of Swanage.

Anvil Point lighthouse, on Durlston Head a mile south-west of Swanage, was built in 1881 by Trinity House and opened by Neville Chamberlain's father, then Minister of Transport. It is positioned to provide a waypoint for vessels on passage along the English Channel coast. To the west it gives a clear line from Portland Bill towards Poole Harbour or the Solent, and to the east guides vessels away from the dangerous Christchurch Ledge to the west. It also marks the hazards of St Aldhelm's Head and Durlston Head.

The small, squat, white-painted circular 39ft lighthouse, with a lantern and gallery, was built to the design of James Douglass and constructed from local stone. The keepers' dwellings were on the landward side. The original clockwork-driven Fresnel lens showed a white flashing light visible for twenty-four miles, but this was replaced when the station was modernised and converted from paraffin vapour to electrical operation in 1960. The lens is now on display in the Science Museum at South Kensington, London. Today a smaller ten-inch lens, consisting of a six-panel fourth order rotating optic, gives a flashing white light which has a range of twenty-four nautical miles.

The explosive fog signal with the jib attached to the lantern was replaced with an automatic Tannoy electric stack in 1971, but this was discontinued in 1988 when a VHF radio signal, operating in conjunction with The Needles, was installed on the roof. The station was fully automated and the keepers withdrawn on 31 May 1991, although a part-time attendant opens the lighthouse for visitors from time to time.

The keepers' cottages, managed by Rural Retreats on behalf of Trinity House, are available for rent as holiday cottages. The lighthouse is situated on the coast path and is a favourite subject for local postcard publishers.

Portland Bill

▶▶ The old high
lighthouse is now
privately owned.

▼ The high light
with the old keepers'
cottages attached.

Portland Bill, at the southern end of the island of Portland, is the most southerly point of Dorset. The Bill is an important way-point for coastal traffic but its position, with the notorious Shambles sandbank just offshore, makes it a major hazard for mariners. The strong tides and currents that form the Portland Race make the area notoriously dangerous for shipping trying to make Portland Harbour.

As a result, providing adequate aids to navigation to mark the Bill was essential and no fewer than three lighthouses have been built at Portland. The first moves to construct a lighthouse came in January 1716 when Trinity House, in response to local petitions, was granted a patent for a pair of range lights to be erected. The lease they granted was for sixty-one years at £100 per annum and the right to collect compulsory dues of a quarter of a penny per ton for

English ships and half a penny per ton for foreign vessels.

The two towers, as well as the anciliary buildings, were completed in September 1716 having been built by Charles Langrishe and Francis Browne. Both towers supported coal-fired lights in glazed lanterns, with the lower light on the east shore marking The Shambles. Maintaining the lights was difficult as access to the southern tip of the Bill was via muddy tracks, and taking coal along these using horse and cart was time-consuming and laborious. As a result, the lights were not completely successful, so when the lease expired Trinity House took over the station.

In 1789 the station was modernised under the supervision of Samuel Wyatt, Trinity House's consultant engineer. The low light was demolished and a new tower was built by Weymouth builder William Johns, who

Portland Bill

▲ The high light after it had been closed in 1906 and the lantern had been removed.

▶▶ The old lower light at Portland has been converted for use as a bird observatory. It was sold by Trinity House in 1907.

▶ The lower lighthouse at Portland when operational, with the two separate houses for the keepers. The one on the right has been demolished.

began work in February 1789. The foundations of the new tower were sited to the east of the existing tower so that it would provide a navigational reference for ships using the English Channel or into Portland Roads, while bringing vessels clear of the Shambles Sandbanks. The new 63ft low light was built from locally quarried stone, and was 20ft in diameter at its base, tapering to 10ft in diameter at the cornice below the lantern.

The coal-fired lanterns were removed, and both towers were equipped with a brand new innovation, Argand oil lamps. Another innovative move was the glass lenses used in the lower light, with the lantern housing six Argand oil lamps positioned inside silvered glass reflectors.

The two Portland lights were 1,509ft apart, with the high light 201ft above high water. The low light was 136ft above high water and had a range of fifteen nautical miles. The cost of rebuilding the towers amounted to £2,000, somewhat below budget, but by the early part of

the nineteenth century the lights at Portland were proving to be very profitable as the level of sea trade was greatly increasing. The net yearly income for 1833 was recorded as £2,300, with the rate set at one penny for English ships and two for foreign.

In 1866 the high light was completely rebuilt and modernised, as was the Low Light the following year, under the supervision of James Walker, and these structures remain today. The high light was a 50ft white-painted circular tower with an attached single-storey service building and two-storey keeper's house. It was fitted with a helical lantern designed by James Nicholas Douglass and manufactured by Chance Brothers of Birmingham. The low light was an 85ft white circular tower with two two-storey keepers' houses nearby. Both stations had three full-time keepers, and each light was visible for twenty-one miles.

During ferocious gales and storms in 1901 about fifteen ships were wrecked

Portland Bill

around Portland, and a better lighthouse was needed. So in 1906, after an appraisal of the cost of operating two lights and the realisation that ships were still being wrecked off Portland, the exitsing towers were closed and replaced by a new tower at the tip of the Bill.

The new tower was designed by Sir Thomas Matthews, Trinity House's Engineer-in-Chief. He designed a tapered circular stone tower with a lantern and gallery. The building work was undertaken by Wakeham Brothers, of Plymouth, who brought several traction engines to the Bill across the rough roads from Portland itself to undertake the contract work.

The tower when completed stood 139ft tall, was painted white with a red band and housed a first order dioptric lens apparatus made by Chance Brothers. The attached service and keepers' buildings were also painted white, and the keepers moved into the accommodation on 11 January 1906. The light was first displayed that evening. The group-flashing catadioptric lens has a range of twenty-five miles and the panels were arranged to give a gradual change from one to four flashes, depending on the direction. The Shambles Reef was marked by a fixed red light through a window.

The old low light is now a bird observatory and the old high light, from which the lantern was removed on decommissioning, a private residence. It has an observation room on top which does not resemble the old lantern. A 29ft obelisk, built in 1844, is located on the cliff edge in front of the 1906 lighthouse and marks the fifty yards long reef which extends out from the Bill. The Shambles Shoal, situated approximately three miles to the east, was marked by two buoys in 1824, then by a lightvessel in 1859. When the red light was erected on the 1906 tower, the shoal was marked with lighted buoys at the east and west ends.

▲ Portland Bill lighthouse cost £13,000 to build.

▶▶ The current lighthouse is one of the most fanous of any operated by Trinity House today.

▼ The lighthouse complex at Portland, with the adjacent buildings now used as a visitor centre.

Portland Breakwater

ESTABLISHED
1857

CURRENT TOWER
1905

OPERATOR
Portland Harbour
Authority

ACCESS
No public access to
either lighthouse
or the breakwater;
they can only be
approached by sea

▶▶ The lighthouse
on Portland
breakwater seen
from the sea.

▼ The Portland
breakwater
lighthouse is at the
main entrance to
the harbour, which
is visited by ships
such as the research
vessel SD Newton.

Portland Harbour is the second largest man-made harbour in the world; it is made up of four breakwaters, two of which stand alone with access only possible by boat. The harbour was first formed by the construction of the two southern breakwaters. Commenced in 1849 by James Rendell, they were completed in 1868 by John Coode. In 1891 a torpedo factory was built in the northern area and between 1893 and 1905 the two northern breakwaters were added.

Originally the harbour was marked by a lighthouse built in 1851 on the northern tip of the outer breakwater. It consisted of a 26ft metal tower, with a lantern that showed an occulting red light visible for six miles. In 1905, when the northern breakwaters were completed, a unique tubular cast-iron tower with hexagonal cast-iron stays, which is the only known survivor of a standard prefabricated tower design, was erected on the southern end of

the North Eastern Breakwater. At 71ft tall, this white-painted tower has a white gallery and lantern topped with a weather vane and shows a flashing white light every two and half seconds, which is visible for ten miles.

In 1914, to improve security against submarine attack, the battleship HMS Hood was sunk across the southern entrance rendering it unusable for shipping. The lighthouse became the main navigational aid for the harbour, marking the more southerly of the two remaining entries. Minor lights are sited on the north ship channel showing occulting green every ten seconds and occulting red every fifteen seconds visible for five miles. The southern ship channel has, in addition to the main light, a quick red light visible for five miles. In March 1995 the navy withdrew from Portland and the harbour is now operated by the commercially operated Portland Harbour Authority.

Teignmouth

ESTABLISHED
1845

CURRENT TOWER
1845

OPERATOR
Teignmouth Harbour
Commission

ACCESS
On the seafront near
southern car park

▶▶ The lighthouse
on the Den at
Teignmouth.

▼ The Phillip Lucette
Beacon at Shaldon,
on the opposite
side of the river to
Teignmouth.

The harbour at Teignmouth was relatively small until in 1843 a new canal, called Hackney Cut, was completed to enable clay barges to get to the mining area around Kingsteignton. This brought clay export trade to Teignmouth, where the entrance into the river Teign over the notorious bar and Pole Sands was extremely hazardous. The bar has a tendency to shift and in fact the entry is so difficult that all vessels are advised to use a pilot.

To guide ships into the river entrance over the Pole Sands a pair of leading lights, on a bearing of 334 degrees, was erected in 1845. The front range, built with the assistance of the Earl of Devon at a cost of £196, consists of a 20ft unpainted conical tower of local grey sandstone situated on the Den near the end of the promenade. The lantern, which houses a fixed red light visible for six miles, is painted blue and has a red weather vane on top. Always operated without a keeper, it was once described: 'The feeble glare emitted from the lantern is of no service by night, except it be to light the fishes to their sandy beds'. However it is still a major aid to navigation 165 years later.

The rear range light, 100ft away, is hard to identify as it consists of a fixed red light, which is visible for three miles, atop a 30ft street light column in front of the Lynton House Hotel in Powderham Terrace. Sector lights, with quick flashing red white lights, and a green light on the Ness headland, guide vessels into the river entrance, where a 15ft metal column is situated on the training wall on the south side of the river entrance.

This white structure with a black base is the Phillip Lucette Beacon and carries an occulting red light visible for three miles in a small lamp holder on top. At the entrance to the harbour is a tall green lattice steel tower on a circular pole called Point Light. This displays an occulting green light four seconds on, one second eclipse, with a fixed green light below in simple lamp holders. Final entry into the harbour is via a pair of leading lights on simple pole structures, which are on the new quay.

Brixham Breakwater

▶▶ The lighthouse
at the end of
Brixham's Victoria
Breakwater.

▼ The breakwater
provides shelter for
a 500-berth marina
situated in the
south-west corner of
the harbour.

Although Brixham has been a significant harbour since medieval times, the first efforts to enclose the area took place in 1690 when King's Quay was built out from the southern side of what is now the inner harbour. The Eastern Quay completed the enclosure in 1760. The construction of the original fish market to the north was carried out between 1799 and 1804.

Although these works provided a safe haven there was a need for further protection and in February 1837 a Bill for a breakwater was considered by Parliament. The breakwater had been designed by James Meadows Rendel and surveyed by C. Greaves in 1836.

Authority for the new and larger Victoria Breakwater was obtained, and the foundation stone was laid in 1843. Due to lack of funds, work stopped at 1,400ft and it appears a light beacon was erected on the end as reports of a storm in 1866, which damaged the end of the breakwater, state 'the beacon on the end was washed away and the local women lit a bonfire to guide their menfolk home'.

In 1909 a 600ft extension was constructed and in 1912 work started on a further 1,000ft extension. When this was completed in 1916, a lighthouse was erected on its terminus. The 20ft white circular cast iron tower complete with a gallery and lantern now shows an occulting red light, electrically powered and visible for three miles.

The fairway into the main harbour is marked by a box light on a pole on the southern promenade, which shows a flashing white light over the channel with red and green sectors to the sides. There is a simple quick flashing white light above it to distinguish it from the apartment lights behind. Entry to the inner harbour is marked by the New Pier Head Light, which is a fixed green light on a tripod.

Berry Head

Berry Head Lighthouse, Brixham

▲ Berry Head was
one of a number
of new lighthouses
built in the early
years of the
twentieth century.
This old photo
shows it shortly
after completion.
It was converted
to unwatched
status in 1921.

▶▶ The small squat
tower is just over
100 years old.

▶ The lighthouse,
58m above high
water, marks Torbay
and Brixham Roads.

Berry Head, designated an area of outstanding natural beauty, is an extensive limestone headland situated just outside Brixham, overlooking Torbay and Brixham Roads, which have long been sheltered anchorages for vessels in the Channel. Fortifications were erected on the headland in 1793 to oppose any invasion by the French, but these were dismantled by 1820 and handed over for civilian use although the ramparts remain, albeit somewhat overgrown.

At the end of Berry Head, beyond the coastguard station, is the small squat circular lighthouse, which is painted in standard Trinity House colours of white with green trim. Built in 1906 under the direction of Sir Thomas Matthews, the 15ft tower was converted to unwatched acetylene operation in 1921 and modernised and converted to mains electricity in 1994.

Berry Head has come to be known as the smallest, highest and deepest light in the British Isles. It is the highest by virtue of its elevation above sea level, the smallest because of the tower's height and small surface area, and the deepest because of the shaft for the rotating lens weight.

Despite being small, the tower is 190ft above mean high water and thus requires no further elevation than that given by the headland. Its light has the character of white group flashing twice every fifteen seconds, and this has a range of fourteen miles. The third order rotating optic is powered by a sixty-watt lamp. It was originally turned by a weight which descended down a forty-five-metre shaft, but when the station was automated it was changed to a small motor.

During October 1942, German planes attacked the coastguard station on the headland and lighthouse, but the damage inflicted was superficial. Sometime before 1875 there was a semaphore signalling post on Berry Head which acted as a Lloyds' signal station for Torbay.

River Dart

ESTABLISHED
prior to 1841

CURRENT TOWER
1981

AUTOMATED
1981

OPERATOR
The Dart Harbour and
Navigation Board

ACCESS
The 1981 light at
Lighthouse Beach is
accessible via a flight
of steps from the
byroad at the top of
Kingswear; the beach
is signed

The old Kingswear
lighthouse was
operational from
1865 to 1980 and
was situated above
the location of the
present light.

The small
cylindrical tower on
Lighthouse Beach
at Kingswear guides
vessels into the
Dart estuary.

The entrance to the river Dart has been fortified since the fifteenth century, when a castle was built on the Dartmouth side. It is not clear when a light was first shown from Dartmouth Castle, but an oil lantern was shown from before 1841 until 1855. A new light was displayed from 1 January 1857, when a fixed red light visible for ten miles was exhibited from a white 50ft square stone tower on the wall of the castle complex.

The light was not a success as the channel was on the other side of the river, and it was discontinued in1865, when a more useful light was erected on the Kingswear side. Some of the lighthouse buildings still exist, however, and can be visited at this English Heritage site.

In 1864 a lighthouse, first exhibited in December, was built within the confines of Kingswear Castle, on the cliffs above. It consisted of a 36ft white-painted hexagonal stone tower with a Chance Bros fourth order dioptric lens which exhibited a red, white and green sectored light visible for ten miles. A sector light on a pole on a rock below showed a fixed white light. By 1980 the tower had become unstable and was demolished, although some remains of it still exist within the castle's grounds.

In 1981 the Dart Harbour and Navigation Board replaced the light with a round 30ft white glass-reinforced-plastic tower, with conical roof. The new tower was erected on Lighthouse Beach, 800 yards upstream from the castle, on the rock where the original sector light had stood. Visible for eleven miles, it shows an isophase white light over the safe channel, with a red sector to the left and a green sector to the right through a window in a square lantern on the dome.

Built in 1864 in conjunction with the Kingswear lighthouse high on the cliffs, about 800 yards inland from the Inner Froward Point headland on the east side of the river, is an 80ft hexagonal granite daymark, which marks the river entrance.

Start Point

Prawle Point and Start Point are two of the most exposed peninsulas on the south coast, running almost a mile out to sea on the south side of Start Bay. This, and the presence of the Skerries Bank to the north-east, resulted in Trinity House's decision in 1836 to erect a lighthouse at Start Point. The lighthouse, designed by James Walker, is situated at the end of the headland and reached via a long winding single track road, hewn out of the rocky ground.

The tower was of a gothic design with a castellated balcony below the lantern room and built with eighty courses of dressed granite. Construction work was organised by Hugh McIntosh, who employed a workforce of about forty men to undertake all aspects of the work, with the granite blocks being brought to the site by sea. The lantern was designed and provided by Alan Stephenson, and was shipped from Leith by steam packet.

Initially, two white lights, first shown on 1 July 1836, were exhibited from the station. The revolving flashing white light in the main lantern room had a range of twenty-five miles and was for passing traffic; the fixed light, shown from a window 23ft below, marked the Skerries Bank. The fixed light was subsequently altered to red, with a range of twelve miles. The main optic, the first of its kind to be used by Trinity House, was a form of dioptric apparatus and displayed a group flashing light three times every ten seconds.

Because the light was found to be inadequate in fog, a bell was installed in the 1860s. The machinery for this was housed in a small building on the cliff face and operated by a weight, which

ESTABLISHED
1836

CURRENT TOWER
1836

AUTOMATED
1993

OPERATOR
Trinity House

ACCESS
Approached via a long service road from Hallsands or the South Devon Coast Path

▼ Start Point lighthouse during the early twentieth century. The flat roofed building was completed in 1844 and the principal keeper's dwelling in front of the tower in 1882.

Start Lighthouse

69

Start Point

▲ Start Point from the air.

▶▶ The impressive lighthouse at Start Point, built in 1836, stands at the end of one of the most rugged and exposed peninsulas on the south coast.

▼ The lighthouse seen from the sea on the peninsula that juts eastward into the Channel.

fell in a tube running down the sheer cliff. A siren replaced the bell after fifteen years. In December 1989 the ground under the fog signal house became insecure and caused the building to collapse. Since then, the site has been levelled, a new retaining wall built, the most southerly keeper's house demolished and the fog signal moved to the main tower.

The 92ft circular stone tower originally accommodated the two keepers and their families on the first two floors, but during the course of the nineteenth century these floors were removed and better accommodation was provided. A flat-roofed north dwelling was built in 1844, to the design of James Walker and built by Weekes of Dodbrooke at a cost of £545, and this was used by the assistant keeper as the principal keeper preferred living

in the tower. Until the 1870s the keeper had just one assistant.

By the end of 1871 the lighthouse machinery had become worn and so Trinity House instigated a thorough overhaul of the station. James Douglass, engineer-in-chief, drew up the plans, which saw the construction of a new three-storey house for the keeper attached to the south side of the tower, and the removal of two of the stone floors in the tower. The work had been completed by 1873 at a cost of £2,800.

The lighthouse was automated in 1993 and the keepers were withdrawn, although a caretaker still resides there and opens the site to visitors at various times found on the Trinity House website. The remaining keepers' cottages are available as holiday lets administered by Rural Retreats on behalf of Trinity House.

Plymouth Harbour

ESTABLISHED
1844

CURRENT TOWER
1844

OPERATOR
Catterwater Harbour
Authority

ACCESS
The Breakwater light
is only accessible
by sea but can be
viewed from the Hoe
and other viewpoints
on the front; Queen
Anne's Battery is
on the other side of
Sutton Harbour from
the Barbican

Plymouth Sound has been a busy centre of shipping for centuries, and as a result numerous small aids to navigation have been built to mark the channels. The port has had naval connections since the sixteenth century and today the city is home to many of Britain's naval ships. Although the most famous lighthouse in the area is Eddystone, for the construction of which John Smeaton rented a field on the west shore of Millbay Creek where he had a workshop for construction of the rock's third tower, some of the smaller lights in the Sound are notable in their own right.

PLYMOUTH BREAKWATER •

Probably the most significant lighthouse in the Sound is that on the breakwater. The breakwater was built during the nineteenth century to improve the safety of vessels waiting at the anchorage to enter port, as bad weather in the bay, particularly from the west, could cause havoc

amongst the sail-powered craft. In 1806 John Rennie and Joseph Whibey designed a 3,000ft long breakwater, 30ft wide at low water, and 10ft above low water. Work began on the project on 12 August 1812. The breakwater had a central section 3,000ft long, with 350ft arms set at 120 degrees to landward at each end; it was 45ft broad and 80ft deep. In 1815 it was increased from 10ft to 20ft above low water.

As the breakwater neared completion there was a need to mark its extremities. In 1813 a light vessel had been stationed off the western end, but it was not sufficient so a proposal was made to erect two lighthouses designed by Rennie, at a cost of £5,600 each, one on each of the arms. However, the western arm was not sufficiently consolidated until 1833 to support the weight and not until 1840 were the foundations for a tower complete by when Rennie's designs were no longer appropriate.

So Trinity House employed Walker & Burgess to design a new lighthouse and building work began on 22 February 1841 on a 78ft tower, 9ft in diameter, constructed of white granite from Luxulyon Quarry. Completed on 9 November 1843, it contained a store room housing a rain water tank, a coal store, an oil room, a kitchen, living and sleeping quarters, an air room where air was collected to feed the burners, and an 8ft tall lantern with an optic of 118 mirrors. It was first lit in June 1844 and shows a white flashing light

▶▶ The impressive Plymouth Breakwater light marks the south-western entrance to Plymouth Harbour.

▶ The lighthouse at Staddon Point (on left) and the beacon at Staddon Beacon mark the eastern entry into Plymouth Sound.

Plymouth Harbour

In a window at 39ft, an additional isophase white light visible for twelve miles shines every four seconds to mark the entrance channel. The lighthouse carries a fog bell, which sounds every fifteen seconds and was acetylene-powered. The light was originally manned by four keepers working in pairs, one month on, one month off.

With the western approach marked, attention turned to the eastern approach. It was not considered cost effective to build a lighthouse so a round beacon, 45ft in diameter at the top which shows three feet above high water, was erected between June and November 1845. Mounted on top is a 17ft pole with a six foot diameter gun metal cage into which six stranded sailors could climb to await rescue.

▲ The light on the north bank of Mount Batten Point at the entrance to Mount Batten Marina.

every ten seconds visible for a mile and a half to guide ships leaving port. A red sector light visible for two miles shows in all other directions.

▶ The light at the root of Millbay Pier shows a quick flashing green light and works in conjunction with a quick flashing red light on the West Pier.

CATTEWATER HARBOUR •
The Cattewater Harbour Commissioners began work on a breakwater from Mountbatten in April 1878 leading westwards towards the Cobbler Buoy. During its construction, a temporary light was exhibited at the end, and plans were made for a proper lighthouse to be built, at a cost of £205, but it is not certain this was ever completed. The breakwater is now marked by two vertical fixed green lights on a red and white banded pole.

The Cobbler Channel is marked by a pair of leading lights, with the rear light on the roof of the two-storey battery building which is home of the Royal Western Yacht Club. The front range is mounted on a red and white banded pole on the inner knuckle of the marina breakwater. Another light, the Catterdown Approach Directional Light, shows a white directional beam, and red and green beams, via a small window from a 20ft circular dome shaped red and white banded tower. The directional light on the south side, called Turnchappel Approach Directional, is similar in design and has the same character.

HAMOAZE • Approaching Hamoaze, vessels pass a series of small pole-mounted beacons off the Bridge headland, before being guided by a directional light at Ravenness. This 40ft white steel tube structure has a small metal gallery mounted on which is a directional light. A directional light at Western King appears to be identical to Ravenness, while the western side is marked by a light at Devil's Point. The main obstacle on the eastern side is the Cremyll Shoal, which is marked by a 20ft square-stepped red stone tower. At St John's Lake, on Sango Island, is a modern red and white banded circular concrete tower supporting a small white light.

MILLBAY DOCKS • The two main lights marking Millbay are at Eastern King, which shows a white light from a window in a metal circular lantern on a white tubular column, and near Millbay Pier, where a directional white light is mounted on a 40ft red and white concrete tower.

PLYMOUTH SOUND • The Sound itself has numerous aids to navigation. The channel between Staddon Point and the breakwater is marked by a light in a small lamp holder on a circular red and white 40ft concrete tower at Staddon Point. To the west is Staddon Beacon, a yellow and white pole in the sea. On the Hoe is the rear range of a pair of range lights, just below Smeaton's Tower. It consists of a 30ft white circular steel tube supporting a small metal lamp. The front range is a similar tube-mounted light in the sea. On West Hoe is a directional light mounted on an oblong 20ft brick structure with the light mounted in a small metal lampholder.

◀ This unique rear range light is displayed from the clock tower of Queen Anne's Battery and shows an occulting red light every eight seconds at a height of 46ft through a square window.

▼ The Rear Leading light on the Hoe below Smeaton's Tower shows an occulting green light and operates in conjunction with a Front Leading light showing a quick flashing white red and green beam on Mallard Shoal, in the sea to the right.

Smeaton's Tower, The Hoe

ESTABLISHED
1759

CURRENT TOWER
1882

OPERATOR
Trinity House

ACCESS
On Plymouth Hoe, open to the public daily in summer as part of Plymouth Dome attraction

▶▶ Smeaton's Tower on Plymouth Hoe, which was used for 120 years until the late nineteenth century. When replaced in 1882, the tower was dismantled stone by stone and rebuilt on the Hoe. It is now painted with alternating red and white bands, and has a white lantern and gallery.

▼ The tower on Plymouth Hoe before the red and white bands had been addeed.

The lighthouse built on the Eddystone reef by John Smeaton in 1759 at a cost of £40,000 was taken down in the early 1880s and now, standing on the Hoe at Plymouth, has become one of the area's best known landmarks. The 72ft circular stone tower had to be replaced on the reef after its base started to be undermined by the sea in the 1880s. So the tower was dismantled and re-erected on the Hoe where it was restored. The stump remains on the reef, fouteen miles from Plymouth, and on a clear day it can be seen with binoculars from the Hoe.

The tower was decommissioned on 2 February 1882 following the completion of John Douglass's tower on Eddystone. As the rocks under the foundations were unsafe, Trinity House was concerned that should the tower fall, it could damage the new tower. It was proposed that the tower should be dismantled and rebuilt on Plymouth Hoe, to replace the Trinity House obelisk that was used to aid shipping in the Sound, and local people raised £12,000 towards the project.

With the consent of Trinity House, work began in October 1882. The first task was to remove the obelisk, which was demolished on 18 October 1882. Two days later the foundation stone was formally laid for the tower by HRH Duke of Edinburgh, Master of Trinity House, and the work of moving the tower to Plymouth began. As removing the tower's base from the reef was impractical, a new base was built using 215 tons of Dartmoor granite, rising in nineteen courses to 20ft 6in. It was identical to the base on the rock, except that an entrance was made at the level of the Hoe.

The portion of the tower above the spiral staircase was then removed from Eddystone and re-erected stone by stone, on the new base. Although care was taken with the rebuilding work, the tower lacked the integrity of the original construction as voids remained where the internal joggle stones had been. Weather bars were also omitted.

The newly moved tower was officially opened and publicly inaugurated on 24 September 1884 by Trinity House's Deputy-Master and Elder Brethren, and stands as a lasting memorial to its builder, John Smeaton.

In 1999, more than a century after it had been erected, the tower was found to be in need of remedial work, so it was encased in scaffolding and refurbishment work was undertaken. The hard non-porous Portland cement used in the reconstruction was cut out from internal and external joints, stones damaged during the rebuilding were repaired and the tower was repointed using breathable lime. Smeaton's covered cornice profile doors and shutters were reinstated, the lantern was refurbished and a replica of Smeaton's chandelier was installed. Replica nineteenth century furniture was placed in the tower, and it was reopened to the public in 2001.

Eddystone

ESTABLISHED
1698

CURRENT TOWER
1882

AUTOMATED
1982

OPERATOR
Trinity House

ACCESS
Can only be viewed
by boat or helicopter

Located fourteen miles off Plymouth in the centre of the English Channel shipping lanes, the rock formation known as Eddystone provides a treacherous obstacle to shipping. Loss of life and cargoes on this hazard in the seventeenth century were only surpassed by those on the notorious Goodwin Sands. The first attempts to mark the hazardous rock were made in 1694, when an agreement was reached between Trinity House and Walter Whitfield, a Devonshire boatbuilder, to build a candle-burning beacon on the rock. But early efforts came to nothing when the huge scale of the project became clear.

WINSTANLEY'S TOWER • The next attempts were made by the eccentric Henry Winstanley who, having had two ships wrecked on the rock, proposed the construction of a light to the Trinity House Brethren. Work started in 1696 to erect

a wooden lighthouse on the highest point of the rock. At the time England and France were at war and one foggy day Winstanley and some of his crew were captured and taken to France. As soon as King Louis XIV found out what had happened, he quickly had the prisoners returned and the privateer thrown into the Bastille. A message was sent by Louis to William II stating 'I might be at war with the English, but not with humanity'. Work then proceeded but with a revised and strengthened foundation, as Winstanley had witnessed at first hand the ferocity of the sea.

Construction progressed slowly until, in 1697, Winstanley decided to increase the working day by living with his crew in the partly constructed tower. On 14 November 1698 a light, using a chandelier of tallow candles, was displayed for the first time in the 80ft wooden tower, and the first tower rock lighthouse in

► The first two lighthouses built on the Eddystone rock were designed by Henry Winstanley and are somewhat ornate in appearance. His first tower (on left) dates from 1698, and the second tower (on right) was built the following year after the first tower had been dismantled. This second tower was 120ft in height, with an 11ft octagonal lantern on top of it.

◀ The third and fourth towers built on the Eddystone rock. The third (on left) was John Rudyerd's tower and this lasted from 1709 until December 1755, when it was destroyed by fire. The fourth tower was that designed by John Smeaton, which now stands on Plymouth Hoe.

the world came into operation. During the first winter, 90ft waves crashed over it, breaking the lantern windows and shaking it so violently that the keepers feared it would be washed away.

In 1699 Winstanley returned and completely rebuilt the lighthouse, increasing its girth to 24ft and its height to 120ft. He also increased the light source to sixty candles. Critics said the light would not last and their comments were to come tragically true in 1703, whilst Winstanley and his men were strengthening the structure. Southern England was struck by a severe hurricane and, when it subsided, nothing could be seen of either men or lighthouse.

RUDYERD'S TOWER • During the four years Winstanley's light was in place, shipwrecks virtually ceased, but they assumed epidemic proportions when the light had gone. In response to pressure from shipowners, Trinity House agreed a patent with John

Rudyerd for a new light, and work began in 1706. Thinking one of the errors in Winstanley's design was the ornate additions which increased resistance to the sea, Rudyerd designed a simple cone-shaped tower and also had a solid stone base constructed, which was 28ft tall.

The new tower stood for forty-six years until the night of 2 December 1755 when, with the keeper attending the candles, an updraft caused the lantern to set alight; within a few hours the whole wooden structure was destroyed. Seeing the flames from the harbour at Plymouth, a Mr Edwards hired a local fisherman to take him out and he managed to haul the keepers from the rock after they had spent a night huddled below the burning structure with debris falling round them. On returning to shore, one keeper ran away and the other, Henry Hall, died twelve days later. It was later discovered he had a seven-ounce piece of lead in his stomach,

Eddystone

► Smeaton's tower on Eddystone was completed in 1759 and stood on the reef for well over a century. This excellent photograph was taken in the latter half of the nineteenth century and shows a Fresnel lens in the lantern.

having swallowed it when the lead roof of the lantern melted.

SMEATON'S TOWER • The consequence of this fire brought about what is now accepted as the most important milestone in rock lighthouse construction – Smeaton's Tower. John Smeaton made a technological breakthrough when he suggested building a solid granite tower which would use its great weight for strength. Hitherto, it had been believed that flexibility was the key to enabling the tower to withstand the extreme forces of the sea, so many doubted Smeaton's idea. But he also used his knowledge of joinery to suggest dovetailing an indent in the underside of each block of granite with a corresponding raised dovetail on the top of the

block below. In this way he could protect the jointing material from the action of the sea.

Work began in August 1756 and, as a temporary measure, a lightvessel was moored two miles north of the rock. With England and France still at war, Smeaton had to obtain an exemption certificate to stop his workforce being press-ganged. One of his revolutionary ideas was to shape the tower like a tree with a curvature at the base which deflected the waves away from the tower, thus reducing the force on it. This principle has been applied to all subsequent rock towers. Smeaton also visited Portland quarries and experimented in the use of crushed limestone and clay to form a substance which, when mixed with sand, produced a paste which dried to form a solid compound. This was then used to cement the blocks, and was the forerunner of Portland cement.

The first granite block was set in place on 12 June 1757 and by 17 August 1759 the last of the forty-six courses was in place, giving the tower a height of 70ft. The lantern was placed on top and, on 16 October 1759, John Smeaton stood on Plymouth Hoe and saw it displayed for the first time. It had cost £16,000 to complete. The light was initially a chandelier of candles, but in 1810 this was changed to oil, and a series of reflectors was installed. Lenses replaced the reflectors in 1845 to give an intensity of 3,216 candlepower.

JAMES DOUGLASS' TOWER • Smeaton's lighthouse remained standing for many years, but by 1877 it was discovered that, although the lighthouse was sound, the rock base below was

Eddystone Lighthouse, near Plymouth

▲ An old postcard of Douglass' tower and the stump of Smeaton's.

◀ The Eddystone lighthouse as depicted in an old postcard before Douglass' tower was modernised. The stump of Smeaton's tower remains in place.

Eddystone

► An engraving showing the formal opening of Douglass' tower on Eddystone on 18 May 1882 by HRH Duke of Edinburgh. The original lantern was constructed of steel covered in gun metal.

►► The Eddystone lighthouse stands fourteen miles off Plymouth. The helipad on top of the lantern was constructed in 1980 and, in 1982, the lighthouse became the first of the major Trinity House lights to be automated when the keepers were withdrawn. The automation was completed and the light reintroduced on 18 May 1982, 100 years to the day after the original opening of the tower.

being undermined. To remedy the situation, plans for a new lighthouse were prepared. James Douglass, Engineer-in-Chief to Trinity House, was sent to the rock and his recommendation for a new tower on a new site on the rock was accepted. Thus began the process of erecting the tower which is in use today.

Having designed the lighthouse, Douglass appointed Thomas Edmonds as resident engineer. Work started on the new tower on 17 July 1878 with the excavation of the rock and construction of a coffer dam which meant the working day could be extended. The coffer dam took a year to complete and, on 19 August 1879, Prince Albert placed various memorials and coins into a cavity below the first stone to be laid. The 168ft granite tower was divided into eight storeys and surmounted by a magnificent 16ft 6in high by 14ft diameter lantern designed by Douglass and built in steel.

The lantern also supported two two-ton fog bells, but these were replaced by a fog gun in 1891. The revolving optic was driven by a weight on a chain which had to be wound by a keeper, an operation which took fifteen minutes in every hour. A secondary light on the fifth level, powered by two Argand oil lamps and reflectors, shone through a window and marked Hands Deep. The lights were converted to paraffin in 1906, which halved fuel consumption and trebled the illumination power.

In 1952 the lights were electrified with diesel generators and 110-volt mercury vapour lamps installed. In 1969, the bi-form optic was replaced by an AGA fourth order catadioptric apparatus, which increased the visibility of the group flashing white light to twenty-two miles.

Casquets

The Casquets rocks lie eight miles north-west of Alderney and present a significant danger to shipping. During the eighteenth century the rocks were owned by Thomas Le Cocq. In 1722 shipowners petitioned Le Cocq to build a lighthouse and offered him half a penny per ton when vessels passed the light. Le Cocq approached Trinity House and a patent was obtained from them on 3 June 1723.

As a distinctive light was needed to ensure it differed sufficiently from those shown from both England and France, three separate towers in a geometrical pattern, making up a horizontal triangle, were proposed. Three towers were erected, each about 30ft high, containing coal fires burning in glazed lanterns. These three lights were called St Peter, St Thomas and Donjon (more commonly known as Dungeon), and were first exhibited on 30 October 1724. The fires were replaced by oil lamps in 1770.

The lease granted to Le Cocq by Trinity House lasted for sixty-one years at a rent of £50 per annum. In 1785, at the end of Le Cocq's lease, the three Casquets lights reverted to the ownership of Trinity House and the brethren introduced various improvements. The lights were converted to house metal reflectors and Argand lamps, which first came into operation on 25 November 1790, and in 1818 a revolving apparatus was fitted to each tower. In 1854 the three towers were raised by 30ft to increase the range of the lights, but in 1877 the North West Tower was raised again and the lights in the other two towers discontinued.

The light was electrified in 1952, while all three towers remain in use, although only the North West Tower now exhibits a light. The East Tower houses fog-signal equipment, which has a range of three nautical miles, and a helideck is mounted on the third tower. The operational tower is 75ft in height, 120ft above mean high water, and the light has a range of twenty-four nautical miles. Casquets was automated in November 1990.

▶▶ The current operational tower at the Casquets has distinctive red and white bands.

▶ An old image of Casquets which shows the three towers, although only one is operational.

Quénard Point, Alderney

Alderney lighthouse, sited on Quénard Point, to the north-east of the island, was built in 1912 to act as a guide to passing shipping and warn vessels of the treacherous waters in the locality. The Alderney Race, a notorious strait of water between Alderney and Cap de la Hague in France, includes the strongest tidal streams in Europe, caused by the tidal surge from the Atlantic building up in the gulf of St Malo and squeezing between Alderney and Cap de la Hague.

Water flows through at speed at high tide and is sucked back as the tide recedes. An uneven seabed adds to the turbulence with further hazardous rocks a few miles offshore. Before the lighthouses had been completed, many ships were wrecked in the area, including the three-masted barque Liverpool, which came to grief on 25 February 1902. She was carrying 6,000 tons of general cargo and was completely wrecked.

The tower itself, complete with lantern and gallery, is 106ft in height with the lantern 121ft above sea level. It is painted white with a central black band to make it distinctive during daylight. The flashing white light, which was converted to electrical operation in 1977, gives four flashes every fifteen seconds and has a range of twenty-three miles. There is also a foghorn which gives a blast every thirty seconds. Two sets of keepers' dwellings and service buildings are attached to the tower by short corridors. The cottages are used as holiday lets.

On 21 June 1940 the keepers and their families were taken from the lighthouse in boats which, after calling to collect the residents of Sark, Casquets and Hanois lighthouses together with some refugees from these locations, safely reached Southampton on 23 June and landed the evacuees. The lighthouse was occupied by the Germans until, after VE day, the keepers returned. They operated the light until 30 September 1997, when it was automated.

▶▶ An aerial view of Alderney lighthouse at Quénard Point. Alderney is only eight miles from the French coast and has just one town, St Anne.

▶ The lighthouse seen from sea, facing the French coast and marking the treacherous Alderney Race.

Point Robert, Sark

The lighthouse on Sark, often referred to as Point Robert because of its location, in an unusual station which, together with the lighthouse on Alderney, acts as an aid to navigation for ships approaching the Channel Islands. Built in 1913, it also guides shipping away from Blanchard Rock a few miles east.

The site is located halfway down a precipitous cliff face; the area was prepared by hewing two flat areas into the rock face, with stone walls supporting the front, together with a rear retaining wall. The two-level flat-roofed service rooms and keepers' dwellings are in a stepped formation. The 55ft octagonal tower has a gallery and lantern rising from the roof of the higher building.

The top of the lantern is a standard drum ventilator on a conical lantern roof rising from the middle of the octagonal tower. The retaining walls are unpainted, while the buildings, tower, gallery and lantern are all white with the standard Trinity House green. Access to the site is via a precipitous flight of steps. Because of its isolated location, the lighthouse was operated as a rock station when manned.

From 1940 to 1945, during the German occupation, the lighthouse keepers were withdrawn and the site was manned by Germans. Two holes were cut into the surrounding walls to form gun emplacements, the area was mined and the store was used as a prison. On 27 October 1945, after the area had been tidied up and two local assistant lighthouse keepers trained, the flashing white light, visible for twenty miles, and the fog signal were again operational. The light and auxiliaries are powered by electricity generated on site.

The only way to visit the site on this car-free island is by ferry from St Peter Port, followed by a walk, bicycle or pony and trap ride to the cliff top at Point Robert. It is then a descent down 165 steep steps to the light itself, which is not open to the public.

▶▶ The lighthouse at Point Robert on the south-east side of the island of Sark.

▶ An old postcard showing the lighthouse at Point Robert prior to automation in 1993.

Les Hanois, Guernsey

▲ Les Hanois lighthouse before the helipad was added above the lantern.

►► The most southerly lighthouse administered by Trinity House, apart from Europa Point in Gibraltar, the impressive Les Hanois lighthouse was built on a reef to the west of Guernsey.

Les Hanois is a jagged reef situated just off the south-western corner of Guernsey on which many unfortunate ships have met their end. Throughout the first half of the nineteenth century local people had been calling for the construction of a lighthouse on the reef, but their approaches to Trinity House in 1817 were rejected by the Corporation. However, the matter did not go away, and by the middle of the century plans were being made for the building of a lighthouse on the reef.

During the 1850s plans for the new lighthouse were confirmed, and in 1859 work on the new tower commenced. It was built to the design of Nicholas Douglass on the largest of the reefs and was intended to guide ships in the English Channel and also mark the Channel Islands.

The novel feature of the tower's construction was the way that the granite blocks fitted together, with Douglass taking Smeaton's methods at Eddystone a stage further. The solid granite blocks were dovetailed both horizontally and vertically. Hitherto, each successive layer of stones had been joined by sockets and pins. But by cementing each block in place, Douglass produced an almost solid tower, and his method became the standard for all future rock lighthouses.

The 117ft tapered granite tower, with seven tiers of accommodation and machinery rooms, was complete with a gallery and lantern. It had a wind vane, but this was removed in 1979 when a helipad was built. In total, 24,542 cubic feet of masonry were used to build the tower, which was 32ft 7in in diameter at the base with the light gallery course 20ft 6in in diameter. The tower cost a total of £25,296 to complete.

The original lantern was a first order optic built and supplied by Chance Brothers of Smethwick. The light was first shown at sunset on 1 December 1862 for two hours, and a week later was officially shone for the first time.

Like other Channel Island lighthouses, Les Hanois was occupied by the Germans during the Second World War and used for solitary confinement. Rumour has it that there is a bullet hole in one ceiling where a soldier or prisoner shot himself. During this time, the large paraffin vapour burner was damaged by gunfire, but in 1964 it was replaced by an electrically-powered fourth order catadioptric optic, with a paraffin vapour burner as standby.

Another couple of notable events at Les Hanois came in 1996 when the tower was the first rock lighthouse to be equipped with solar power, and on 4 January that year it became the last rock station to be automated and demanned. At this point, the rotation of the light was reduced, changing the character of the light from two flashes every five seconds to two every thirteen seconds, which enabled the length of the flash to be increased, thus retaining the existing range of twenty miles.

Platte Fougère, Guernsey

ESTABLISHED	1910
CURRENT TOWER	1910
AUTOMATED	1950
OPERATOR	Guernsey Harbour Authority
ACCESS	Can only be visited by boat

The light at Platte Fougère lies just over a mile offshore, but can be seen from Fort Doyle. The fog signal gives one blast every forty-five seconds.

The Russell Channel which leads into St Peter Port is strewn with rocks such as Grande Braye, Brasier and Platte Fougère. It also has a treacherous tidal race. After local ship owners spent many years petitioning the States, the island's Parliament approached David and Charles Stevenson for advice. As the Parliament could not afford a full scale lighthouse, they suggested an automatic light and fog signal, choosing Platte Fougère rock as the most suitable location.

Situated about a mile offshore near the north-easterly point of Guernsey, the lighthouse was completed in 1910. Managed by the Guernsey Port Authority, it consists of an 82ft octagonal concrete tower painted white with a single black band. The foundations, situated almost entirely under water, were of Portland cement cast in iron moulds and strengthened with iron bars. One of the two rooms is for the motors and air compressors and the other has this equipment duplicated. With no lantern, the apparatus on top consists of a light. Prior to 1950 acetylene tanks and a fog signal were also in operation.

Modern additions include a Racon beacon and solar panels. The light, which shows flashing white with a flashing red sector towards Grande Brayes, is visible for sixteen miles. When built in 1910, the fog signal was operated by electricity via a submarine cable from Fort Doyle, but the light was acetylene gas powered with supplies delivered by boat. In 1950 the light was converted to electrical operation.

St Sampson, Guernsey

The harbour of St Sampson, to the north of St Peter Port, was developed in the eighteenth century for the export of granite from the nearby quarries. In 1790 a breakwater was built out from Mont Creviet to form what is now the outer harbour, which is still used for commercial traffic even though it dries out at low tide. The inner harbour was constructed in the mid-nineteenth century and today houses a yacht marina.

The channel into the harbour is marked by a pair of range lights, the front of which is situated on Crocq Pierhead. Probably erected in 1874, it is a 20ft cast iron tower, with a domed roof, mounted on a stone base which houses an equipment room. A fixed red light with a range of five miles shines through an oblong window.

In 1874 a building, originally the harbour master's office, was positioned at the rear of the harbour so that the rear range light could be shown from there. Mounted in the copper-domed roof of the clock tower, the fixed green light has a focal plane of 42ft and a range of five miles.

ESTABLISHED
1874

CURRENT TOWER
1874

OPERATOR
Guernsey Harbour Authority

ACCESS
Both lights can be seen from the road, and the lights are situated on the public land

◀ The front range light at St Sampson is displayed from the red-painted circular tower on Crocq pierhead; the rear range is shown from the copper-roofed clock tower at the rear of the harbour.

St Peter Port approaches

ESTABLISHED
Brehon Tower 1856
Roustell Tower 1923

CURRENT TOWER
Brehon Tower 1856
Roustel Tower 2002

OPERATOR
Guernsey Port
Authority

▶ Brehon Tower, to
the north-east of St
Peter Port, can only
be reached by boat.

TAUTENAY • Of the lights operated by Guernsey Harbour Authority to mark the Little Russel Channel between Herm and Guernsey, the most northerly is Tautenay. Originally a daymark, this 23ft stone tower situated to the north-east of the channel is painted with black and white vertical stripes. The original daymark probably dates from the nineteenth century but the small light on top is of modern design. It is only accessible by boat.

BREHON TOWER • The Brehon Tower, situated about three miles north-east of St Peter Port, is an

old circular stone fort built by Thomas Charles de Putron on a rocky outcrop. The fort was occupied for about fifty years and was used by German troops during the occupation. As early as 1744 a seamark had been established on Brehon Rock, but after complaints that it was not very clear, a 40ft mast was erected as a replacement. The light, built in 1856, is situated on top of the fort and shows an isophase white light having been built to replace a pyramid sea marker. Operated by Guernsey Harbour Authority, it marks the Little Russel Channel. The

▶ St Martin's Point
light and Longue
Pierre Beacon

northern approaches into St Peter Port are via the Little Russel Channel running between a number of rock outcrops. Transit A, bearing of 208 degrees, requires the light on Brehon Tower to be aligned with the light at St Martins Point.

PLATTE • The Platte light, situated on the west side of the channel to the north-east of St Sampson, was originally a nineteenth century daymark consisting of a bright green 30ft conical stone tower; it is now fitted with a modern navigation light, which gives a red flash landward and a white flash seaward. Vessels approaching the channel from the north have to use one of three transits to safely proceed through the area. Transit C, bearing 198 degrees, requires the lights on Roustel Tower to be aligned with Brehon Tower after which Transit B is required.

ROUSTEL TOWER • Roustel is a concrete tower located on a rock off Herm. Erected in 1923, it was demolished after being hit by the motor vessel Winchester in February 1970. A 26ft triangular steel lattice tower was erected on the base of the original tower later that year. In 2002 the tower was rebuilt and now the concrete base is painted in a black and white chequered pattern. The tower carries a black vertical day mark. The quick flashing white light is visible for seven miles.

ST MARTIN'S POINT • At the south eastern tip of Guernsey, this light is displayed from a short post on the roof of a single storey 17ft square white-painted building. It shows a white light, flashing three times every ten seconds, which is visible for ten miles, and has a small red sector. It is sometimes referred to as Jerbourg Point. The main Transit B requires the St Peter Port Front Range light on the end of Castle Breakwater to be aligned with the Rear Range at Belvedere.

ST PETER PORT FRONT RANGE (CASTLE BREAKWATER) • Described in detail on page 96.

ST PETER PORT REAR RANGE (BELVEDERE) • Situated on a wooded hillside just to the south of St Peter Port is a 10ft white circular steel tower with a domed roof. The tower has an occulting white light, visible for ten miles, which shines through a window near the top. On either side of the tower is a slatted white daymark with a white concrete base.

▼ Belvedere light on the hill overlooking Havelet Bay.

St Peter Port, Guernsey

St Peter Port is the main harbour on Guernsey and the island's ferry port. Vessels are guided in by a light on Castle Breakwater at the south side of the entrance. Called Castle Breakwater Light, or more accurately St Peter Port Harbour Front Range, it consists of a 40ft tapered circular granite tower and a lantern with a conical roof.

The outer facing side of the tower and lantern are painted white, with the gallery black, to act as a daymark. The electrically-powered light, which like all the lights around the harbour is operated by Guernsey Port Authority, shows a fixed white light followed by a fixed red. The rear range, called Belvedere, shows a white occulting light from a short metal tower on the hill behind the harbour and gives a bearing of 220 degrees. Nearby at Belvedere House is a fixed white light.

The light on the North or White Rock Pier is displayed from a tower built into the end face of the pier wall and supported by an inverted stepped base. The 36ft circular stone tower has a small entry door halfway up, with a set of steps, and a walkway along the top of the harbour wall gives entry to the light. Located in a white dome-topped lantern, the electrically-powered optic shows a flashing green light.

Adjacent to the car park on the North Quay is a directional light on a 30ft four-legged wooden tower with an octagonal lantern topped by a weather vane. The structure is white, apart from the two seaward sides of the lantern, which are red. The electrically-powered optic shows a narrow fixed white light with a quick-flashing green sector to the north and quick-flashing red sector to the south. All the lights are accessible on foot.

▶▶ The most significant aid to navigation at St Peter Port is the impressive Castle Breakwater light.

▶ This unusual tower is built into the pier wall on the end of White Rock or North Pier at St Peter Port harbour.

La Corbière, Jersey

ESTABLISHED
1874

CURRENT TOWER
1874

AUTOMATED
1976

OPERATOR
Jersey Port Authority

ACCESS
Via a causeway, which is only passable at low tide after which a klaxon sounds to warn visitors to return to the mainland

▶▶ La Corbière lighthouse was originally attended by four keepers, who lived in the nearby cottage, but after automation they were withdrawn.

▼ The seas off La Corbière are treacherous, with many outcrops of rocks and a vicious tidal race.

The lighthouse at La Corbière is perhaps better known for its picturesque location than its history. Situated on an outcrop of rocks six miles east of St Helier, it guards the shipping routes between Guernsey and the British Isles. Built in 1874 by Imre Bell to the plans of Sir John Goode, the 62ft white-painted tower was the first concrete lighthouse in the British Isles. That it has withstood the savage seas in this exposed spot, with virtually no damage since, is a testament to its design and construction.

The light, maintained by French lighthouse authorities, has an isophase light with both red and white sectors visible for eighteen miles. Originally paraffin oil-fired, it was converted to electricity and the keepers removed in 1970. Access to the lighthouse is via a causeway which is only passable at low tide. All the materials for the construction of the causeway, the tower and the service building were transported from St Helier by barge and landed on a lower working platform by jackstay. The mixed concrete was raised to the site by an inclined railway and the tower was cast in situ. The light, first shown on 24 April 1874, is 119ft above mean high water, giving it a range of eighteen miles.

During the Second World War the lighthouse was camouflaged. The light was dimmed on 4 September 1939 and extinguished in June 1940, remaining so for the duration of the German Occupation until it was relit on 19 May 1945. On 28 May 1946 the keeper Peter Edwin Larbalesrier lost his life saving a holiday-maker who remained too long on the causeway. A plaque at the landward end of the causeway marks his life.

The station had a fog signal sounded by a bell with an explosive detonator; this was replaced by a compressed air horn in 1933. During automation an electric fog signal giving four blasts every minute was installed.

Noirmont Point, Jersey

ESTABLISHED
1915

CURRENT TOWER
1915

OPERATOR
Jersey Harbours

ACCESS
Best viewed from the cliffs above; it is possible to walk to the tower at low tide, but only with extreme caution

▼ Noirmont Point light is shown from a squat tower sited at the western end of St Aubin's Bay.

To the east of St Aubin's Bay on Jersey's south-west coast lies the rocky headland of Noirmont Point. The estate in which it is located was originally retained by the Duke of Normandy, but in 1946 it was purchased by the States of Jersey and is now a memorial to those who gave their lives in the Second World War as well as various historic exhibits and a memorial stone. It is also the site of a Napoleonic tower, which was built between 1810 and 1814 to defend the island against Napoleon, as well as a series of German bunkers, which are maintained by the Channel Islands Occupation Society.

Noirmont is the most southerly point on Jersey and its rocky outcrops are a major hazard to seafarers passing from La Corbière to St Helier. To aid mariners, in 1915 the Napoleonic tower was fitted with a light to mark the Sillettes Reef about a mile to the south. The light, mounted on this 32ft high stubby tapering stone tower, originally supported a lantern, but this was later replaced by a polycarbonate lamp on a short mast.

In recent years it has been refurbished and converted to solar power, and today the electrically-powered light is mounted on a small square pedestal on top of the black and white banded tower. The light, operated by Jersey Harbours, gives four white flashes every twenty seconds and has a range of thirteen miles.

The tower is situated on a rocky outcrop, which in theory is accessible by wading at low tide, but this is not advised.

Demie de Pas, Jersey

The area south of St Helier harbour is strewn with rocks with a buoyed channel through them. The most southerly is Demie de Pas with Danger Rock and Fairway Rock to its west. Vessels approaching from the east must pass outside the rock before turning into the channel.

In 1904 the Jersey Harbour Authority marked the obstacle by erecting a 44ft cone-shaped concrete tower to guide vessels entering the harbour. Originally it was painted white with a gallery and a lantern but, in about 1984, the lantern and gallery were replaced by a small navigation light. The base of the tower was repainted black and the upper part orange. In 2002 the RAF funded a new solar-powered light, fog signal and radar beacon. This increased the height as it was mounted in a circular tube on top of the cone.

The area inland of the light is hazardous so the white flashing light shows a red sector over 180 degrees to landward. The white light has a range of fourteen miles, and the red ten miles.

ESTABLISHED	1904
CURRENT TOWER	1904
OPERATOR	Jersey Harbours
ACCESS	Can only be viewed by boat

◄ The tower at Demie de Pas after modification in 2002, with a fog signal which gives three blasts every sixty seconds.

La Grève d'Azette, Jersey

ESTABLISHED
1896

CURRENT TOWER
1896

OPERATOR
Jersey Harbours

ACCESS
Approached from
St Helier via the
promenade, and
situated on the beach

Vessels approaching St Helier harbour from the west have to pass between Noirmont Point lighthouse and Les Fours buoy before altering course in line with a pair of range lights, which guides them through the channel from Noirmont Point towards Dog's Nest beacon, before aligning with the leading lights into St Helier harbour.

The front range, called La Grève d'Azette, is about a mile to the east of the harbour on the sea front. Built in 1896, the solid concrete base is built into the promenade sea wall and the 64ft high lattice steel tower has a gallery and a lantern with a hooded light. The white-painted tower has a red daymark on the side facing the sea.

The electrically-powered light shows an occulting white beam at five-second intervals, visible for fourteen miles. During daylight the light can be used in conjunction with the Dog's Nest Beacon, situated to the east of the harbour entrance. At night it is used in conjunction with the rear range light at Mont Ubé.

▶ La Grève d'Azette light on the beach adjacent to the promenade and the A4 main road.

Mont Ubé, Jersey

Vessels approaching St Helier harbour from the west have to pass between Noirmont Point Lighthouse and Les Fours buoy, before altering course in line with a pair of range lights which guides them through the channel from Noirmont Point towards Dogs Nest beacon prior to re-aligning with the leading lights into St Helier harbour.

The rear range called Mont Ubé, is situated someway inland on the top of a hill in St Clements just over one mile to the north east of the La Grève d'Azette Front Range. Built in 1896, the 46ft white lattice steel tower on a concrete base has a gallery and lantern with a hooded light. It shows an electrically-powered red light occulting every five seconds, visible for twelve miles.

During daylight hours, because of its location, Monte Ubé is not effective as a daymark, so the front range at La Grève d'Azette is used in conjunction with the Dog's Nest Beacon. During hours of darkness, the Mont Ubé light is used together with the front range.

ESTABLISHED
1896

CURRENT TOWER
1896

OPERATOR
Jersey Harbours

ACCESS
Situated on a minor road between the A4 and A5 roads, on the way to Le Hocq

◄ Mont Ubé Rear Range light is situated on a hill in the St Clements district of Jersey.

St Catherine's, Jersey

ESTABLISHED
1856

CURRENT TOWER
1950

OPERATOR
Jersey Harbours

ACCESS
At the end of
St Catherine's
breakwater, which is
open to the public

The development of the harbour at St Catherine's came about during the 1840s as a result of rivalry between Britain and France. The government and Admiralty decided to build large naval bases on Jersey and Alderney. St Catherine's on Jersey was chosen for one of these harbours, just fourteen miles from France. The intention was to build a 1,200m northern breakwater which would sweep round towards a southern breakwater projecting from Archirondel. This would form a large harbour of refuge, second only in size to that at La Havre.

Work began in 1847 and eight years later 640m of the northern breakwater had been completed. But bad weather and lack of finance delayed the project and, as the British and French were now allies, no further work was carried out. The southern arm had only just been started, and all that remains of it is a small pier.

A lighthouse, sometimes known as Verclut Breakwater Head, was imported into the island on 5 November 1856 and by 12 December 1856 had been installed on the end of the breakwater. It consisted of an ornate eight-sided 30ft metal tower which showed a flashing white light visible for eight miles. This tower was replaced in 1950 by a modern square 25ft lattice tower with an open platform from which a small light shows a white flash every one and half seconds, visible for eight miles.

The original lighthouse is now on display outside the Jersey Maritime Museum in St Helier. A plaque on the tower, dated 9 November 1996, reads: 'Apart from the five years of German Occupation this light, from St Catherine's Breakwater shone brightly for over 100 years to warn seamen of danger. Today it stands as a monument to those islanders who died in concentration camps far from their island home. A symbol of remembrance and a beacon of hope for the future.'

▶▶ The nineteenth century lighthouse from St Catherine's Breakwater outside the Maritime Museum in St Helier.

▶ The modern light at the end of St Catherine's Breakwater shows a white light.

Sorel Point, Jersey

ESTABLISHED
1938

CURRENT TOWER
1938

OPERATOR
Jersey Port Authority

ACCESS
Car park nearby, then short walk down a coastal path

▶▶ The unusual black and white lighthouse at Sorel Point.

▼ Sorel Point is situated on the most northerly tip of Jersey.

Situated on the most northerly headland of Jersey, Sorel Point is dominated by the huge Ronez Quarry, which occupies its western side. The point itself faces the Normandy coast to the north and offers good views towards France and Sark. However, the Paternoster Reef and its associated dangers, which lie to the north west in the direction of Sark, and Les Dirouilles, a range of rocks to the north east, provide a serious hazard to seafarers passing down the French coast or from Guernsey and Sark.

To guide vessels through this dangerous area, a lighthouse was constructed in 1938 on the east side of the headland. Built by Jersey Harbour Authority, it was housed in an unusual 10ft semi-circular concrete pillbox with a flat concrete roof. Operating on acetylene gas, the light originally shone through a long window, which was later altered to a small square lantern on the roof and later still to a yellow lantern.

At the turn of the last century the complex was reconditioned and converted to solar power. The solar panels were located on the roof so the lantern was again positioned inside the building, with the optic showing a rotating light through the long window. There are two white sectors with red sectors marking the Paternoster Reef and Les Dirouilles Rocks formed by red panels across two of the window panes, thus giving a red and white flashing light with a character of two seconds on and five and a half seconds eclipse.

With its distinctive black and white chequered squares, the building also acts as a day mark.

Gorey, Jersey

ESTABLISHED
1849

CURRENT TOWER
1966

OPERATOR
Jersey Port Authority

ACCESS
Gorey pier is open to
the public, and the
light is easily reached

During the seventeenth century Gorey was the main harbour on Jersey although in 1685 Dumaresq wrote that the pier was old and decrepit. However, it was not until 1815 that a decision was made to rebuild it, and by 1817 the stone pier, which is still in existence, had been completed.

In 1849 a fine hexagonal stone tower lighthouse, approximately 30ft in height, was erected on the end. It stood on a raised pedestal and was topped by a coned-shaped lantern with a gallery. This lasted until 1964, when disaster struck and the whole structure fell into the sea.

In 1966 a new light was displayed from a 30ft white square skeleton tower with a small red lantern showing a green or red light. This was the front of two lights, with the rear range consisting of a red occulting light on a 3ft square white panel with an orange surround, mounted on Mont Orgueil (Gorey Castle) 1,600ft away. The rear range is no longer operational, and the light on the pier flashes on one second, eclipse four seconds.

▶ The small square tower at the end of Gorey pier, marking the entrance to the small harbour, housing a flashing light, which has red and green sectors.

Grosnez Point, Jersey

Grosnez Point, on the north west corner of Jersey, is the first sight of the island for visitors from England or the other Channel Islands . While not as famous as the La Corbiere lighthouse four miles to the south, the light at Grosnez is important as its red sector marks the dangerous Paternoster Reef to the north east.

Jersey Port Authority erected a light on the headland in 1948, shown from a 6ft square 7ft tall white concrete hut with the light in a cylindrical lantern. In the late 1990s this structure was replaced by a 9ft white oval metal column with a small double polycarbonate lantern on top. The flashing light has both white and red sectors visible for nineteen and seventeen miles respectively.

Immediately after the German Occupation, twenty six guns were dumped over the point. Two have been recovered and it is hoped more will be found.

ESTABLISHED
1948

CURRENT TOWER
prior to 2000

OPERATOR
Jersey Harbours

ACCESS
Car park nearby, then short walk

◄ The original Grosnez Point light was in use from 1948 to the 1990s.

▼ The site of the light at Grosnez Point is on the edge of the Les Landes SSI and bird watchers also come to the area.

Glossary

▲ Start Point.

▲ Newhaven breakwater light.

▲ The lantern in Hurst high light.

Acetylene A highly combustible gas which burns with an intensely bright flame.

Argand lamp A bright and relatively clean-burning lamp invented by Francois-Pierre Ami Argand in 1783.

Automated An unmanned light controlled externally; all the major UK lighthouses are automated with Trinity House controlling and monitoring its lights from the Corporation's Depot in Harwich.

Beacon A structure, usually land based, either lit or unlit, used to guide mariners.

Character The identifying feature of a lighthouse is its character; for example the light could be described as fixed, or flashing.

Daymark Light towers often also serve as daymarks, which are fixed unlit beacons visible from the sea and marking a navigational hazard.

Dioptric lens A development by Augustin Fresnel consisting of a bull's eye lens surrounded by a series of concentric glass prisms. Dioptric lenses were classified by the focal length.

Elevation The elevation refers to a light's height above sea level; the higher the elevation, the greater the range.

Flashing light A light where the period of light is less than the period of darkness.

Fog signals A sound signal, often located with a light, used to warn mariners in times of fog or heavy weather.

Gallery The external walkway encircling the lantern.

High light The taller or higher of a pair of lights.

Isophase light A light where the periods of light and dark are equal.

Keeper The person responsible for maintaining and keeping the light at an aid to navigation, including the associated buildings.

Lanby The abbreviated term for Large Automatic Navigation Buoy, a modern floating unmanned aid to navigation often used in place of a lightship.

Lanterns The glass-enclosed space at the top of a lighthouse housing the lens or optic; lanterns are often encircled by a narrow walkway called the gallery.

Lightship A vessel, powered or unpowered, designed to support a navigational aid.

Low light The shorter or lower of two lights used to mark a channel or hazard.

Occulting Where the period for which a light is exhibited is greater than its period of eclipse; this can be achieved in several different ways.

Range lights Lights in pairs which mark a channel.

Reflector A system which intensifies light by reflecting the light source into a beam, both to increase intensity and to enable the beam to be manipulated to produce differing light characteristics.

Training wall A bank or wall erected below water level in a river or harbour mouth to train the water flow.

Appendix

Bibliography

Boyle, Martin: Lighthouses of England and Wales: Beachy Head (B&T Publications, 1999).

Boyle, Martin and Trethewey, Ken: Lighthouses of England and Wales: Needles Point (B&T Publications, 1996).

Dafter, Ray: Guernsey Sentinel: The Remarkable Les Hanois Lighthouse (Matfield Books, Tonbridge, 2003)

Hague, Douglas B. and Christie, Rosemary: Lighthouses: Their Architecture and History (Gomer Press, Dyfed, 1975).

Merrett, L. H.: Smeaton's Tower and the Plymouth Breakwater (Maritime History, Plymputh, Vol.5, No.2).

Nicholson, Christopher: Rock Lighthouses of Britain (Patrick Stephens, Somerset, 1995).

Sharp, Eric W.: Lighthouses of the Channel Islands (Guernsey Historical Monograph No.17, St Peter Port, 1979).

Woodman, Richard and Wilson, Jane: The Lighthouses of Trinity House (Thomas Reed Publications, 2002).

▲ Portland low light.

Websites

www.alk.org.uk Association of Lighthouse Keepers; unique archive, a museum at Hurst Castle, quarterly Journal.

www.lighthousedepot.com Comprehensive list of world lights with details, photos, locations and links.

www.trabas.de/enindex.html List of world lights including minor lights with photos.

www.unc.edu/~rowlett/ lighthouse/index.htm Comprehensive list of world lights with photos and links.

www.trinityhouse.co.uk Trinity House website with details of all their lighthouses.

▲ Hurst low light on the wall of the castle.

Acknowledgements

A number of people have assisted with this book and we gratefully acknowledge those who have supplied information and images for inclusion. All photographs are by Nicholas Leach, except Tony Denton 28, 32 (left), 33 (lower), 43, 52, 75, 109 (upper); Association of Lighthouse Keepers (ALK) 16; Trinity House 11 (upper); John Mobbs 5 (lower), 7, 8 (upper), 10 (upper), 11 (lower), 22, 36, 40, 42, 56 (upper), 56 (upper), 58 (upper), 70 (upper), 76, 81, 90; Andrew Cooke 5 (upper), 50; Michel Forand 6, 14, 31, 47; Ian Lamy 12, 92, 101; FotoFlite 39; Mat Dickson 49; Paul Dalloway 60, 61; Mike Millichamp 80; Brian Green 1, 9 (upper), 85, 87; David Ham 64; Ken Trethewey 78, 79, 110 (middle); Tony Rive 89, 91, 93, 94, 95; David Wilkinson 110 (bottom). Thanks also to Gerry Douglas-Sherwood of the ALK and Paul Howe of Trinity House. Finally, our gratitude extends to Maureen and Sarah for their support and patience during the preparation of this book.

▲ The light on the walls of Southsea Castle.

Index